There is lots to like [...] that David Rosebe[rry...min]istry as the rector of his congregation. It's super! I'm glad to have read it, and I commend it to both clergy and lay leaders.

The Right Rev. John Guernsey

This book will be revolutionary for those who will take the time and read it and then act on it! I thought it was well done . . . and extremely well-thought out. I usually work with para-church ministries—never with a church itself—but this book is a game-changer for both! Thank you, David!

Todd Dexter, TDA Associates

Fantastic! This is not only David's best book, but this may be the best book written on this subject. It really hits on all areas of church needs. It's a winner!

Ben Gill, founder, Resource Services, Inc.

David's book is great. He is clear, honest, and thorough. In my career of working with hundreds of pastors and churches, I would have given this book away many times over. It is a great resource.

Richard Caperton, Capital Campaign Consultant

Let's face it, very few lay people and even fewer clergy get into ministry to put together the next stewardship campaign. In this book The Rev. David Roseberry, perhaps for this reason calls the ministry of giving the "third rail." Yet it's why this book is so completely valuable! A step-by-step, biblical, practical, and winsome approach to transform your church through healthy generosity. This is a must read! Bravo, David!

> **The Rev. Alfred T.K. Zadig Jr.**, rector, St. Michael's Church, Charleston, SC

David has been a trusted guide for many over the years on the topic of stewardship, for me included. I've sought out David's counsel on this topic many times. I am delighted this book captures it so accessibly for others. It is a book you will likely find yourself dog-earing pages, marking up, and revisiting as you tackle this needful topic in the life of any congregation.

> **The Rev. Andrew Petta**

The case can be made that the New Testament job description of bishops and presbyters is to preach the Gospel and raise funding for ministry. This field guide will encourage lay and ordained persons with practical steps for leading others to giving generously. David Roseberry first taught me these principles for a "Heritage 2000" Building Campaign that exceeded all goals and raised $2.5 million dollars years ago and for two other successful projects since then. We continue to use his teaching in our annual giving at St. Mark's, Geneva. I am grateful for his wisdom that has helped me with that New Testament call for leaders to create enthusiastic donors for God's work.

The Rev. Mark Tusken, Rector, St. Mark's, Geneva, Illinois

We are living in challenging times where many churches are facing financial strain and pastors are struggling to find resources that will help them teach and preach on stewardship. Look no further. Based on biblical principles and decades of practical experience, David Roseberry's timely *A Field Guide for Giving* will help pastors and churches teach on the blessing of giving in today's complex world.

Dr. Winfield Bevins, author, *Liturgical Mission* and *Ever Ancient Ever New*

David Roseberry has a deep understanding of biblical teaching on generosity and stewardship that he offers to readers in a very practical and winsome way. After having helped thousands of congregations to grow disciples and fund billions of dollars for ministry, I am glad to have this book in print. I highly recommend it!

Joe Park, CFRE, Horizons Stewardship

A FIELD GUIDE FOR GIVING

INCREASING GENEROSITY IN THE LOCAL CHURCH

DAVID H. ROSEBERRY

Copyright © 2022 David Roseberry

All rights reserved. No portion of this book may be reproduced, stored in a retrieval system, or transmitted in any form or by any means—electronic, mechanical, photocopy, recording, scanning, or other—except for brief quotations in critical reviews or articles, without the prior written permission of the publisher.

Scripture quotations marked (ESV) are from the English Standard Version. Copyright © 2001 by Crossway, a publishing ministry of Good News Publishers. All rights reserved

ISBN Paperback 978-1-7358461-5-6
ISBN eBook 978-1-7358461-6-3

Book cover design by David Roseberry and BluDesign, Nashville, TN
Interior design by YouPublish (youpublish.com)

Published by RML Books, 4545 Charlemagne Drive, Plano, Texas 75093

Printed in the United States of America

CONTENTS

Introduction 9

1. Beginning the Journey 15
2. The Bible: The First Field Guide 27
3. The Apostle Paul: Wealth Advisor 37
4. The Prosperity Gospel? 47
5. Talking About Generations 57
6. Preaching Stewardship 67
7. Developing Stewards in the Church 81
8. Estimate of Giving Cards 97
9. Budget Basics and Year-End Giving 113
10. Funding Capital Projects or Improvements 127
11. Inside a Capital Campaign 133
12. Best Practices of a Generous Church 145
13. Why Generosity? 159

INTRODUCTION

Dear pastor, minister, or church leader:

This book is a practical field guide to the world of Christian stewardship in our modern culture. Field guides help travelers identify flora, fauna, landmarks, and other natural features in an environment and along a journey. That is how I hope you will use this book. This book will help you identify issues, avoid hazards, appreciate landscapes, understand pitfalls, and safely navigate the challenging trails as you lead and teach stewardship and generosity in your local context.

The church's approach to stewardship and generosity has enormous implications for the spiritual health and growth of the people of God. A church needs to get beyond mere fundraising and bill paying. As we can all imagine, it is possible to raise a lot of money and, at the same time, damage the spiritual lives of our flocks in the process. There is a higher calling here.

It is better, and longer lasting, to teach the ways of biblical stewardship and generosity. When the people of God see the blessings and opportunities provided for them, they will grow in their faith and knowledge of our Lord. They can become more like Him—which is the primary goal of Christian ministry. Who among us pastors, having served the church and pastored people, cannot relate to Paul's plea to the Galatians? He was both emotionally passionate and deeply perplexed when he wrote "*My little children, for whom I am again in the anguish of childbirth until Christ is formed in you!*" (Gal. 4:19).

I sincerely believe that right teaching and good practices within a congregation can assist mightily in forming Christ in people and transforming people into the image of Christ (2 Cor. 3:18).

LAYOUT OF A FIELD GUIDE FOR GIVING

To start our journey well, let's inventory our tools and prepare for some common challenges in our path. Here is how this book lays out:

- Chapter 1 - Why leaders are often reluctant to talk about money with their congregants—and why it's too important not to!
- Chapter 2 - A biblical and early Christian understanding of money and generosity from the Old Testament through early Church history.
- Chapter 3 - A deep dive into the Apostle Paul's comprehensive teaching about stewardship found in his letters to the Corinthians.

- Chapter 4 - The modern Prosperity Gospel phenomenon and how church leaders can effectively respond.
- Chapter 5 - How different age groups and think about and respond to stewardship teaching and fundraising efforts in the local congregation. Each generation holds a very different viewpoint.
- Chapters 6 - How to teach and preach on stewardship and generosity. This chapter will help you think creatively about the communication task.
- Chapter 7 - Specific talking points when interacting with members and donors face-to-face. This is an unusually anxious topic for pastors. We'll demystify the process and help you have fruitful and faithful dialogue with those who can support the mission of your church or organization.
- Chapter 8 - The sticky wicket of pledge cards, online giving, ETF, ACH, and estimate of giving options. Each church has its own unique needs, and no one system fits all. The pandemic has brought many options to the forefront.
- Chapter 9 - Year-end giving plans and budgeting issues. Many of these plans can be implemented in the last six weeks of the calendar year.
- Chapter 10 - How to introduce capital campaigns—essential to helping a church or organization pay for large projects.

- Chapter 11- Inside the workings of a capital campaign, including a list of necessary items to consider before launching any fundraising.
- Chapters 12 - An overview of all the best practices discussed in the book and thoughts on why generosity should be understood and practiced by every church member. Best practices are simply ideas that seem to work well in congregations. I hope some of them are helpful to you.
- Chapter 13 - A message that will encourage you to continue the challenging journey of ministry and the essential work of teaching stewardship and generosity.

My denominational background is Anglican. I was ordained an Episcopal priest in 1983 and planted Christ Church (Episcopal) in the fall of 1985. For many reasons, our vestry voted to leave the Episcopal Church and join the Anglican Church in North America in 2006. Most of the Anglican terms (rector, senior pastor, vestry, etc.) have their counterparts in the wider church in the United States and Canada. I am sure that you can translate and adapt anything from this book into your own tradition and background. I hope pastors and church leaders from all Christian traditions will find this field guide helpful.

This is my second book on generosity. The first one, *Giving Up*, came out in 2017, and I am so thankful to have had the encouragement of many pastors to keep writing. A few of the ideas in this guide were first introduced in *Giving Up*, but in the ensuing years I have had more time to develop them and see them work successfully in other congregations.

I pray that these books will help you develop the subject of generosity for your leadership board and congregation. Further, I hope this field guide lives in your hip pocket or on an eye-level shelf on your bookshelf as you navigate and enjoy the road of stewardship.

May God bless you as you lead your church on a journey to generosity!

— The Rev. David H. Roseberry,
Executive Director, LeaderWorks

1

BEGINNING THE JOURNEY

By definition, a field guide introduces you to the place you want to go. As you begin the journey, a field guide will tell you what you need to know, why you need to know it, and what things look like along the way. Are there dangers ahead? Are there warnings to heed? Are there wonders to see that will make the journey exciting and rewarding? How should you prepare for the journey? A field guide should answer all these questions.

Also, a field guide should be short enough to carry in your back pocket but thorough enough to cover the most important material. Given the content of a field guide, and the wisdom it can convey, a field guide can be a ready companion along the way.

I hope that this book will do these things (and more) for you.

Let us begin.

WATCH OUT FOR THE THIRD RAIL

If you board a subway in any large city, then you likely will see the warning signs: "Do not touch" or "DANGER! Keep clear of the third rail." The train's wheels run on two harmless outer steel tracks. A third rail, sometimes in the middle or off to the side in a shrouded cover, runs along the track. It is electrified. That is where the power is; that is where the subway finds the means to move down the track. Without that third rail, the car will sit motionless.

But if you ever touch that third rail, beware! It could give you the shock of your life—or the last shock of your life!

In a church setting, speaking, teaching, leading, and preaching about money can similarly be like a third rail—*necessary but hazardous*. We all agree that a ministry needs funding through tithes and offerings to fuel its mission, just as a subway train needs electricity to move. Yet when it comes to broaching the subject of giving, let alone teaching it, many pastors can become anxious, numb, and silent.

The rare leader who works up the nerve to talk about financial stewardship can sometimes be in for a surprise. If he boldly goes where few pastors have gone before, he might get zapped. Regular givers might shift uneasily in their seats. Members who do not tithe or give at a sacrificial level (and sadly, many do not) will struggle with guilt. Some will feel disconnected, even shut out. Guests will roll their eyes. Too often, it is feared, they might not come back!

Over the years, I have coached and counseled dozens of pastors, lay leaders (called vestries in the Anglican Church), and leadership boards. Most have collected an often-quoted list of good reasons to avoid the topic of stewardship. I have heard and seen them all:

- "Frequent teaching on generosity gives the impression that we are always asking people to give."
- "We need to stay clear of too much money talk, or visitors will feel uncomfortable."
- "Our pastor doesn't know who tithes or how much a person gives." (Note: While noble, this "hands-off" approach handcuffs the pastor. Because he doesn't know the congregational stewardship practices, he cannot teach effectively.)
- "We should delay teaching on stewardship. Our discipleship process must first focus on freshmen-level subjects, such as prayer and social outreach. Advanced studies, such as financial giving, can come later."
- "When people read the Bible, they will see that they should give. We do not need to remind them. God will. After all, tithes and offerings are between God and the giver."

These are relevant points. Yet how will people know about biblical giving if they are not taught? How can they grow if they are not challenged? How can a ministry move forward without the power of generosity?

For a church to have the power it needs to move, for the members of the church to have the knowledge and understanding of their role as stewards in God's creation, and for the senior pastor to teach diligently the whole counsel of God, we must get comfortable working with the third rail.

To begin our discussion, let's visit a church I call St. Archimedes. Wait, what? St. Archimedes?

Read on.

A LEVER AND A PLACE TO STAND

As a young boy, I was enthralled by all sorts of pulleys, wheels, and simple machines. When I discovered Archimedes' Lever—in the third grade or so—my world expanded. Archimedes was a mathematician in ancient Greece. Famously, he once said, *"Give me a lever and a place to stand, and I will move the earth."*

What a powerful statement!

Archimedes was not a Christian, of course. He could not have been; he lived hundreds of years before the Lord was born. Thus, he never attended church. He probably never visited a synagogue either. Nonetheless, his maxim can and should inspire Christian leaders. Why?

Perhaps the English philosopher G. K. Chesterton had Archimedes in mind with he offered this compelling maxim: *"We do not want a church that will move with the world. We want a church that will move the world"*

As clergy and lay leaders, we want to see the world moved by the power of the Gospel and the love of God.

On what shall we stand? On God and His Word, of course. In Him, we have a firm foundation, a solid rock.

And what is our lever? At its best, a local congregation is the lever for the gospel. Indeed, through the teaching and preaching of the Gospel, the local body of Christ is the best lever we have! It alone can lift the world in a God-ward direction. Nothing has more power to effect change and impact people than the church when it's functioning, focused, and well-funded. It is a thing of indescribable beauty. It has exponential strength. And when a church is clear about its message, its mission, and its methods, it has unlimited potential.

It is not too much to quote John Wesley on the same subject:

> *Give me one hundred preachers who fear nothing but sin and desire nothing but God, and I care not whether they be clergymen or laymen, they alone will shake the gates of Hell and set up the kingdom of Heaven upon Earth.*

This is the unbridled strength of a local body of Christ—no other organization on earth can compare. Its people and its ministries are a lever that God uses to draw whole communities, families, and people toward Himself.

ST. ARCHIMEDES CHURCH

St. Archimedes, a fictional church, is a model of a local church serving as a lever at work changing the world.

Picture a healthy congregation of two hundred or so worshipers in attendance on a typical Sunday. That's St. Archimedes. One full-time and three part-time staff members run the place on an annual budget of about $300,000. Somehow, they offer a full complement of church programs: youth ministry, Sunday school, adult Bible studies, nursery care, a women's group, community outreach, mentoring for mothers with young children, an annual summer camp for neighborhood youth, and more. St. Archimedes also provides monthly support for a local food bank, donates space for an afterschool tutoring ministry, and hosts two substance recovery groups. Oh, I almost forgot to note: they fund two overseas missionaries.

In short, St. Archimedes leverages its modest attendance, staff, and budget to make a powerful impact on its members, the community, and the world. Here are a few outcomes over a ten-year period:

- More than two hundred children have learned the basics of scripture and the creeds in Sunday school and youth ministry, giving them a solid foundation for their lives.

- Business leaders, teachers, salespeople, government employees, skilled laborers, office staffers, and all sorts of workers attended an adult Sunday school, then took the biblical principles they learned back into the marketplace, blessing countless thousands.
- Through local food banks, homeless programs, battered women's shelters, and more, church members touched hundreds of individuals and families who never appeared on Sunday morning attendance rolls.
- The church's missions program constructed four church buildings in a developing country and funded the drilling of six freshwater wells in another.
- Dozens of new believers attended small group Bible studies that enabled them to deepen their faith and create a sense of fellowship. They became members of the church community, which provided emotional and spiritual support during tough times.
- Three teens who committed to Christ at summer camp later went into full-time ministry. They planted three churches in different areas of the city.

St. Archimedes' pastoral staff provided marriage and family counseling, personal mentoring, burial services, baptism and confirmation preparation, Christian instruction, crisis intervention, hospital visitation, various Bible studies, theologically sound sermons, spiritual support for dozens of families, a rapid response team for local emergencies, community input, significant times of prayer, and more.

Impressive! The church helped move many people and the community toward God. That small congregation changed their world—and it continues to do so. How? The leverage started with the pastor. He regularly taught his members to be good stewards. He didn't shy away from candid talks about giving money and time. His vestry supported the message, and the members embraced it. Week after week, they tithed, gave offerings, and volunteered their time. To the glory of God, generosity became a core part of St. Archimedes' DNA.

I created the story of St. Archimedes as an ideal model. But every pastor can see similar outcomes—if he or she enables God's people. I know. I was one of those leaders who faced the dilemma of whether to teach stewardship or not.

Permit me to tell my story.

GRAB THE THIRD RAIL AND HANG ON!

A few years after I graduated from seminary, I was involved in starting a new church and teaching about money fell to me. I had studied at a modern seminary, but stewardship was never taught there. My only real-world ministry model was horrendous. Faced with the need to fund our ministry, I had no clue what to do.

Like many other church leaders, I feared that any mention of giving tithes and offerings would scare off people. Our church plant was growing; people were excited to be a part of God's work. I didn't want to break the momentum; consequently, financial stewardship was the last thing I wanted to talk about.

For years, I downplayed generosity. I preached about money, but my sermons were lackluster at best; I found that I was trying hard *not* to sound like a salesperson. In those days, teaching about and practicing biblical stewardship was not fundamental in our denomination—it was incidental. And soon enough, our young congregation paid the price for my neglect.

Then, the bottom started to fall out. Sunday morning attendance growth noticeably slowed. After five years, it stopped cold. Even in our thriving Texas community, we were stalled. I began to fear that our best days were behind us.

Complicating matters, we had just purchased land and constructed a building. Adding real estate principal and interest payments to our normal budget squeezed us. Our vestry favored scaling back programs, trimming the staff, and paying off the new building over twenty years. I grew sick to my stomach with the thought. That was "death by amortization." As unsavory as it was, however, it was a better plan than dividing the budget between the members, as my previous boss had done. I was not sure what was God's plan.

One evening at our regularly scheduled vestry meeting, a lay leader suggested we take a different approach. Richard was a mid-level manager at a large software company. He had studied the congregation's budget, the record of giving, and our growing shortfall.

One evening, as we pored over a depressing budget report, Richard spoke up. "I don't think we have an expense problem," he said. "We have an income problem. We don't need to cut; we need to grow! And we need to teach stewardship."

Richard's words rang true and captured my imagination. I began to see giving as a critical aspect of Christian discipleship. My approach to generosity would need to change dramatically. And it did. Radically.

First, I stopped being so sheepish about how to meet the church budget. I ceased apologizing for bringing up the "sensitive subject" of money. I was no longer embarrassed or afraid to speak out. I knew I needed to bring the entire church on board, so I scheduled a four-week series on biblical stewardship.

To prepare, I studied scripture and prayed hard. Then I announced to the church in advance that I would speak on a biblical vision of money—their money.

Would my announcement scare people off? I knew that it might, but I was excited. My reluctance had disappeared. When Sunday came to launch the series, I was shocked. Attendance was up!

Teaching biblical stewardship for the first time was powerful. It moved our congregation forward. Year after year, I approached giving and generosity with a more profound conviction. With each sermon, the people grew in their understanding too. They came to a greater awareness of how God could use them to advance the mission of Christ and His Church. I reached out and grabbed the third rail of church ministry. And I am alive to write about it.

I didn't know much when I started on my biblical stewardship journey. I certainly didn't see that money, giving, generosity, and sacrificial offerings were recurring themes in the Bible. Furthermore, I had no clue about the power this third rail would bring to ministry. Subsequently, attendance, giving, staff, and enthusiasm grew beyond my expectation.

That is my story. I was one of the first converts to my own preaching about the good news of giving. Since then, it has been a journey for me that has been as surprising as it has been exciting.

In the next chapters of this book, walk with me as we embrace a lever that can change the world.

2

THE BIBLE: THE FIRST FIELD GUIDE

I wrote *A Field Guide for Giving* to be a companion for any Christian leader and congregation leading their church on a journey toward generosity. You will find ideas, suggestions, best practices, and principles that can work in any Christian tradition or denomination. However, it is not the first field guide on the subject. There is another book that is the primary source, the ultimate guide, and the inspiration for this short companion book. The Bible is the original field guide and everything that is written in the book you have in your hands—every "takeaway" from it—is subject to and conditioned upon agreement with the first book, the Scriptures of the Old and New Testament.

Most people reading this book could have written this chapter on the Bible's approach to stewardship. The chapter is not exhaustive. It cannot be—the Bible is the best book on the subject, and it speaks volumes about it. However, let's take some time to refresh our understanding of stewardship, generosity, and the Bible.

Early in my ordained ministry days, I recognized the Word of God as that firm foundation. Indeed, somewhere along the path of ministry I was told that the Bible is the best book on the most important subjects. This aphorism has stood the test of time. Scripture gives us all we need to know about money, time, resources, giving, generosity, tithes, and offerings—everything that falls under the umbrella of stewardship.

The Scriptures are awash with principles and stories of faithful giving and living. In Old Testament times, Jewish people had this primary practice engrained in their religion and culture. They learned about sacrifice; they learned about offerings. Likewise, first-century Christians held clear convictions regarding use of money and time.

The Bible doesn't present stewardship as an advanced subject only for upper-level students.

Instead, giving, generosity, and stewardship is regarded as general education, foundational to life. As pastors and leaders of modern congregations, we should treat it the same way.

In other words, stewardship should not be a back-burner issue. Any church that doesn't make giving a clear priority does a severe disservice to its members and its mission. A pastor who avoids regular and repeated teaching, preaching, writing, and studying on the topic is missing a vital part of the life of faith.

KEY VERSES

As mentioned, the Scriptures take a robust and most positive approach to stewardship. It's not taboo. There isn't a third-rail mentality (or whatever the ancient equivalent of a third rail would be). Instead, as faithful disciples of Jesus, we are instructed to know how to use the funds, skills, talents, and time God gives us to benefit His Kingdom. Let's look at a handful of examples (among many hundreds) of passages.

The Bible teaches us that giving is:

A Sign of Trust and Confidence in God. The Scriptures forbid believers from "putting God to the test" (see Deut. 6:16; Luke 4:12). Put another way, we must not insist that God prove Himself trustworthy. We simply must have faith that He is. Yet in the last prophetic book of the Old Testament, the Jewish people (and we) are directly invited to test God in the arena of giving. We are to give generously, and then wait to see how God gives back in abundance. This is different than demanding God prove Himself to us. Instead, it is an opportunity for Him to demonstrate His faithfulness when we obey.

> *Bring the full tithe into the storehouse, that there may be food in my house. And thereby put me to the test,*

> *says the* LORD *of hosts, if I will not open the windows of heaven for you and pour down a blessing until there is no more need. (Mal. 3:8–10)*

An Expression of Worship. Transformation happens on many levels after our Lord claims and restores a person upon conversion. Among the changes: that person becomes a giver. In the Sermon on the Mount, Jesus touched on spiritual generosity. Our Lord taught that when we worship publicly, we should present a gift to Him. (This is true whether we give our time to ministry, a tithe as an offering, or a song as an act of worship and praise.)

Jesus further emphasized the centrality of worship when He taught us to make personal amends with others before presenting a gift or an offering to the Lord.

> *So if you are offering your gift at the altar and there remember that your brother has something against you, leave your gift there before the altar and go. First be reconciled to your brother, and then come and offer your gift. (Matt. 5:23–24)*

Jesus went on to say that giving to others in need (which are also acts of worship) should be private, seen by the Father alone:

> *When you give to the needy, do not let your left hand know what your right hand is doing, so that your*

> *giving may be in secret. And your Father who sees in secret will reward you. (Matt. 6:3–4)*

Thus, both public and private acts of worship are aspects of giving in obedience to Christ.

An Investment in the Future. In Luke's version of the Sermon on the Mount, called the Sermon on the Plain, Jesus described the principle of reciprocity behind giving: *"Give, and it will be given to you. Good measure, pressed down, shaken together, running over . . ." (Luke 6:38).*

Then, in 2 Corinthians, the Apostle Paul quoted Jesus as saying, "*Whoever sows sparingly will also reap sparingly, and whoever sows bountifully will also reap bountifully" (2 Cor. 9:6).*

These two ideas, brought to us by Jesus and then by Paul, are a fascinating intersection. Paul seldom (almost never) quoted Jesus directly. But in these instances from Jesus' Sermon and Paul's letter to the Corinthians, we hear an echo of the same idea: giving is an investment in God's generosity for the future. We will talk about the so-called Prosperity Gospel later, but for the moment, I am just stating the obvious, agreed-upon understanding of Jesus and Paul: giving is never like a one-way street. It is reciprocal. It comes back to the giver in some way.

The Way of Jesus. Within the Early Church and throughout the centuries, generosity has been a hallmark practice of Christians. First-century Christians voluntarily gave of their bounty to support the poor, widowed, and people in need. Luke the Evangelist wrote about these acts of love: *"And they were selling their possessions and belongings and distributing the proceeds to all, as any had need" (Acts 2:45).*

The first Christians fully embraced the idea of "taking up a collection" for those among them who were in need: *"The disciples determined, every one according to his ability, to send relief to the brothers living in Judea" (Acts 11:29).* Paul even gave specific instructions to the Christians at Corinth on how this should be done.

This courageous and habitual generosity of the Early Church stood out in stark contrast to the brutality of the Roman Empire. Christians of that day were so counter-culturally generous that they became famous for it. Two generations later, in the year CE 125, a Greek philosopher and convert to the Christian faith named Marcianus Aristides described the standard practices of his fellow Christ-followers:

> *Christians live in hope and expectation of the world which is to come. So they do not embezzle what is held in pledge nor covet what is not theirs. If one or other of them has servants or enslaved people, through love towards them, they persuade them to become Christians, and when they have done so, they call them brethren without distinction.*
>
> *They love one another, esteem widows, and rescue orphans from any who ill-treat them. Whoever has wealth gives to him who has not, without boasting.*

When they see a stranger, they take him into their homes and rejoice over him as a very brother.

Whenever one of their number who was poor passes from the world, each one of them contributes to his burial according to his ability. And if they hear that one of their numbers is imprisoned or afflicted on account of the name of their Messiah, all of them anxiously minister to his necessity, and if it is possible to redeem him, they set him free. If there is among them any that is poor and needy, and they have no spare food, they fast for two or three days to have food that they can supply to the needy.

Echoing Aristides, retired New York pastor and author Tim Keller draws a sharp distinction between the Greco-Roman world of greed, lust, and power and the Christian behaviors of giving, compassion, and grace:

The Early Church was strikingly different from the culture around it in this way—the pagan society was stingy with its money and promiscuous with its body. A pagan gave nobody their money and practically gave everybody their body. And the Christians came along and gave practically nobody their body, and they gave practically everybody their money.

Biblical Models. The Scriptures have more to say about stewardship and everything under its umbrella. Depending on what words you include (*silver, riches,* etc.), the Word mentions money as often as two thousand times. As a sampling, consider how many significant leaders and teachers in the Bible grab the third rail:

- Jacob pledged 10 percent of whatever God gave him as a tithe to God (see Gen. 28:20-22). Setting aside the first 10 percent of our income for God—what Christians widely practice today, with variations of understanding—was firmly established later in the Mosaic law. This gift belongs to God, not the giver (Lev. 27:30).
- King David acknowledged and praised the source (God) of his people's giving and generosity: "*But who am I, and what is my people, that we should be able thus to offer willingly? For all things come from you, and of your own have we given you*" (1 Chron. 29:14; also see vv. 10–19).
- The teacher who collected the sayings in Proverbs included the observation that "*a generous person will prosper; whoever refreshes others will be refreshed*" (11:25, NIV). Who doesn't want to prosper? Who doesn't want refreshment? To prosper, we must first give.
- A little-observed fact in the life of Jesus is that He took an interest both in what people gave and how they gave it. Remember the story of the widow's mite in Luke 21:1–4? Jesus made it His business to notice not just the amount people gave but their attitude in sharing it.

- Paul coached young pastor Timothy to touch the third rail on purpose! He told his protégé to stand up to the wealthy patrons in Ephesus and warn them about putting their trust in riches (see 1 Tim. 6).
- Writing to the Christians in Corinth, Paul compared their slow pledge payments for the believers in Judea with the overwhelming generosity of the Macedonian churches (see 2 Cor. 8–9). We'll look more closely at this passage in the next chapter.

Indeed, one of the most comprehensive teachers about money and giving should not surprise us. The Apostle Paul was transformed by Jesus Christ on the road to Damascus, and it was not just his mind and heart that were changed. Every aspect of his life fell under the influence and power of the Holy Spirit—including his understanding of money.

As mentioned above, save for an occasional reference or passing phrase, the incredible ministry of the Lord Jesus is barely mentioned in any of Paul's letters or sermons—*except when it comes to money.* There is a quotation (above) about sowing and reaping in 2 Corinthians. This phrase is an echo of what Jesus taught in the Sermon on the Plain (Luke 6:38, quoted above).

Then in a conversation with the Ephesians elders recorded in Acts, Paul quoted a saying of Jesus that is not recorded in any of the four Gospels! Paul, facing his friends from Ephesus whom he would never see again, said, *"Remember the words of the Lord Jesus, how he himself said, 'It is more blessed to give than to receive'" (Acts 20:35).*

Stewardship is one of those subjects in the Bible that hides in plain sight. It is everywhere, but it is also overlooked everywhere. However, once you see it, you cannot "unsee" it.

In the next chapter, let's go back to the great Apostle Paul and examine his stewardship awakening.

3

THE APOSTLE PAUL: WEALTH ADVISOR

As we all know, the Apostle Paul, alongside the Holy Spirit, played a leading role in the New Testament story of the Early Church. Paul planted more than a dozen churches and traveled extensively in Asia Minor, Macedonia, and Greece. From there, over centuries, the Gospel would go forward. Indeed, aside from Jesus Christ Himself, no other person impacted world history as significantly as Paul.

As recorded in Acts and through many of his epistles and pastoral letters, Paul had a clear sense of stewardship and generosity and did not hesitate to teach and explain it to the churches he pastored. He gave profound advice, doctrinal teaching, correction, counsel, encouragement, and warnings to the earliest Christians—and a significant share of his words show how to think about money and possessions.

No field guide to giving would be complete without reference to his teaching. Let us look to the Apostle to the Gentiles for his advice.

BACKGROUND CHECK

Prolific as Paul was, we know very little about his childhood, upbringing, and genealogy. He was a Roman citizen (see Acts 22). That means there's a good chance he was raised in a wealthy family. Because he was Jewish, his father or grandfather likely purchased their status (citizenship often cost at least eighteen months' wages).

Paul described himself as a tentmaker (see Acts 18). In the ancient world, this profession did not have the blue-collar ring it does today. Jews were enmeshed in the textile industry in Tarsus, Paul's hometown. They made high-quality dwellings (tents) and even saddles. His family might well have been industry leaders there.

Like many children from wealthy families, Paul received an elite, private education; in his case, it was at the feet of the renowned Rabbi Gamaliel (see Acts 22). Most Jewish families of that day could never afford such a luxury.

What about Paul's business dealings and adult life? Again, we have only scant details. Paul's letter to the Philippians, written from prison in Rome, indicates he experienced a wide range of financial conditions in his life. A history of dramatic changes seems to be behind his well-known statement about self-sufficiency and God:

> *I have learned in whatever situation I am to be content. I know how to be brought low, and I know how to abound. In any and every circumstance, I have learned the secret of facing plenty and hunger, abundance and need. I can do all things through him who strengthens me. (Phil. 4:11–13)*

Was Paul raised in wealth? How much privilege did he lose when he became a Christian? We cannot be sure. We do not need to peg the history of his social standing—he never did. However, other than his skill as a tentmaker, when he became a Christian on the road to Damascus, he lost whatever financial and social position he enjoyed in his early years. But it never seemed to make a difference.

A FRIENDLY FUNDRAISING RIVALRY

His early life aside, Paul seemed to have an open hand and pure heart regarding money. He was comfortable asking for support as needed but refused to take compensation for his work on other occasions so as not to *"put an obstacle in the way of the gospel of Christ" (1 Cor. 9:12).*

How did this play out? In Acts 9–10, after Paul regained his strength and recovered from the trauma of his conversion, members of the church in Antioch disciple him. His enthusiasm to launch an evangelism strategy grew. Soon enough, Paul volunteered, along with Barnabas, to lead the first mission trip.

As Paul traveled, he preached the gospel. Along the way, he raised money for his brothers and sisters in Jerusalem, who were suffering from a famine. Paul did not hesitate to ask for money (see 2 Cor. 8–9). There was no third rail to watch out for! On the contrary, as a pastor he boldly went where few pastors had ever gone before. To raise money for the Christians in Judea, he devised a brilliant fundraising strategy.

Since this is a field guide, I need to add a caution at this point. Paul's method to motivate the Corinthians to give generously and fulfill their pledge touched, with both hands, the third rail completely. I would advise modern pastors to imitate Paul's passion, but not his plan. You have been warned!

First, to meet the need in Judea, Paul laid out how much the Christians in Corinth should give. Unlike the pastor I worked with early on, who equally divided the church's budget by the number of families, Paul directed each family to provide based on what they earn. He instructed church members to donate in proportion to their income: *"Now concerning the collection for the saints: as I directed the churches of Galatia, so you also are to do. On the first day of every week, each of you is to put something aside and store it up, as he may prosper" (1 Cor. 16:1–2).*

The believers in Corinth made a pledge. They knew some of the leaders in Judea by reputation (1 Cor. 1:12). They admired them. I am sure they wanted to support the cause. So they enthusiastically made a commitment to give.

But they were pokey-slow in fulfilling it. To motivate the Corinthians to fulfill their pledge of support for the suffering Judean Christians, Paul boldly challenged them to give above and beyond their neighbors to the north in Macedonia, effectively setting up a fundraising rivalry between the two churches.

> *We want you to know, brothers, about the grace of God that has been given among the churches of Macedonia, for in a severe test of affliction, their abundance of joy and their extreme poverty have overflowed in a wealth of generosity on their part. For they gave according to their means, as I can testify, and beyond their means, of their own accord, begging us earnestly for the favor of taking part in the relief of the saints—and this, not as we expected, but they gave themselves first to the Lord and then by the will of God to us. Accordingly, we urged Titus that as he had started, so he should complete among you this act of grace. But as you excel in everything—in faith, in speech, in knowledge, in all earnestness, and in our love for you—see that you excel in this act of grace also. (2 Cor. 8:1–7)*

Imagine the outcry we would hear in many churches today if a leader tried a similar tactic? Yet Paul didn't apologize for this boldness—not one iota. Neither should we; instead, we need to be confident. How can Paul's strategy be modified or adapted to be more workable for Christians today?

ADVICE FOR A YOUNG PASTOR

As good as Paul was at raising funds to help the needy, his grasp of giving was much more expansive (and profound). Timothy and the church he led in Ephesus discovered this firsthand.

When Paul warned against idolatry in Ephesus, riots erupted. When he preached the gospel of salvation, a revival broke out. Perhaps because of these dramatic events, Paul took a direct interest in his protégé Timothy and the health of the church in Ephesus. He loved his brothers and sisters there, and the feeling was mutual. There remains even today a likeness of Paul painted on a cave wall outside the ancient city. Indeed, in one of the most touching moments in Acts, Paul said goodbye to the church elders before he left for Jerusalem, and they all wept together.

This evidence of such deep mutual love provides a necessary backdrop to help us understand Paul's encouragement to Timothy to deal firmly with wealthy members of his congregation. Residents of Ephesus from all walks of life responded to Paul's (and Timothy's) life-giving message and joined the church. Some newcomers were business leaders in the community. Their success in commerce perhaps made them a bit bossy, even entitled.

Sound familiar? This happens far too easily among people who have been financially successful.

But Paul saw the problem that Timothy had and offered some advice. He told Timothy to stand up to these well-off Christians and to warn them firmly but lovingly of the possible consequences of loving wealth:

> *Those who desire to be rich fall into temptation, into a snare, into many senseless and harmful desires that plunge people into ruin and destruction. For the love of money is a root of all kinds of evils. It is through this craving that some have wandered away from the faith and pierced themselves with many pangs. (1 Tim. 6:9–10)*

Later in the same chapter, Paul spelled out the instructions he wanted Pastor Timothy to pass along to the wealthy among his church members:

> *Charge them not to be haughty, nor to set their hopes on the uncertainty of riches, but on God, who richly provides us with everything to enjoy. They are to do good, to be rich in good works, to be generous and ready to share, thus storing up treasure for themselves as a good foundation for the future, so that they may take hold of that which is truly life. (1 Tim. 6:17–19)*

Is this how you talk to your wealthier church members? I need to ask myself this question, and probably you do too.

A MODEL TO FOLLOW

In this brief overview of Paul's teaching on finances, we see a man who, while he may have had wealth at some point, grew beyond a need for it. He could take or leave it. Because he didn't lust after material gain, he could challenge beloved church members and friends to think rightly about their relationships with money and giving.

When we survey the instructions that Paul gave the Early Church concerning money, we can see that Paul imagined money in four different categories.

Greed. First, he knew that money was the source of the means of personal greed. This is evident in the firm instructions he gave to Timothy regarding the wealthy and their love of money. Greed turns us into a monster that wants more and more stuff, and at the same time, greed becomes a monster that wants more and more of us! There is abundant evidence of this in our culture: the more we strive for possessions, the more they possess us.

Feed. Second, Paul knew that money should be used to supply ourselves with enough to eat. In this way, it is like our feed. Paul was aware that all of us need money to live and provide for our families. He was seriously critical of the freeloaders in Thessaloniki who were so convinced of the imminent return of Jesus that they stopped working. *If a man will not work, he will not eat* (2 Thess. 3:10)! Paul was a realist about money. It is useful for food. It is our feed.

Need. Also, Paul understood money in a compassionate way. Money is useful to fulfill a need in another person's life or for another church or community. In a sense, the financial collection for the saints in Jerusalem was the subtext for the missionary travels of the Apostle Paul. There was a human need. There was a crisis in the land. People needed money to buy food.

Seed. But finally, and wonderfully, Paul understood that money functions as seed. Giving money is like investing in a future, eternal crop. The seed goes in the ground, and it yields an abundant harvest. This "seed" use of money is the highest and best use of what's in our wallets, to be sure. This is the exact point that Jesus made in the Sermon on the Plain.

In sum, Paul didn't see the topic of money and ministry as inappropriate or uncouth. It's not high-pressured or awkward. He is upfront and honest about it. He boldly placed his hand directly on the third rail and didn't let go.

BUT WHAT ABOUT . . .

I want to add a qualification at the end of this chapter on Paul and his theological understanding of money. As bold as he seemed to be about touching the third rail, there was an overarching sensitivity to the reputation of the Gospel, and frankly, his own reputation. Paul was clear about money. He gave financial advice. He encouraged others to give. He even gave a handy method of determining the amount they could give and what to do as their own resources increased.

But Paul was painstakingly aware that, in asking for money—or God forbid—demanding payments and compensation for services, ministry, and travel, he might cause others an offense. In some places, Paul asked for money to support the ministry and then in other settings, he refused to ask for help. In Romans 15, Paul said that the Gentiles owed money to the Judeans and yet, in the same sentence, he backed away from any mention of his personal need. Why? It might be because Paul had never met the Christians in Rome. The reputation that would have preceded his visit might have been damaged or compromised. May it never be! N. T. Wright wrote this about Paul's financial request made in Romans 15:

> *I sense in Paul what I see in myself and in a great many others: a reluctance even to raise the topic at all, and then a sense of nervousness in what we say, lest we at any point we should be misunderstood.*[1]

---

1. *Romans for Everyone*, 126–7.

4

THE PROSPERITY GOSPEL?

A field guide like this must include a discussion of the most provocative but popular idea in the modern church. Any pastor who teaches biblical stewardship today will inevitably encounter what is loosely called the "Prosperity Gospel." A growing contingent of Christians embrace some form of this money-centric doctrine.

The Prosperity Gospel is rooted in the belief that once Christ redeems us, we have a divine right to health and wealth. Proponents teach that through the atonement, we should enjoy not only sin's defeat but the end of sickness and poverty in our lives.

Looking through a temporal lens, who wouldn't want this to be true? The reasons for its growing popularity and worldwide spread are evident. The Prosperity Gospel promises the giver a better life, more money, more excellent health, and blessings upon blessings amid the world today. It all sounds like the American dream. And that is where it came from.

Prosperity teachers draw from a uniquely American notion that fuses capitalism, consumerism, and Christianity. And to make matters even more complicated, along with much of our pop culture, the Prosperity Gospel is one of our most popular exports. The practice of linking our Christian faith to our personal finances is preached around the world. The hope and promise are this: as faith goes up and we show more and more evidence of faith in how and what we give, our finances will increase as well.

But like most gnostic heresies and others like them, the idea is based partly on biblical truth, partly on flawed human reasoning, and partly on a self-centered quest for pleasure. Unfortunately, unscrupulous leaders can use this teaching to fill their coffers and severely disappoint people's sincere desires for God's blessing in their lives.

FIRST WE GIVE, THEN WE GET

In Chapter 3, we looked at a passage from the prophet Malachi:

> *Bring the full tithe into the storehouse, that there may be food in my house. And thereby put me to the test, says the LORD of hosts, if I will not open the windows of heaven and pour down for you a blessing until there is no more need. (3:10)*

Jesus said something similar: *"Give, and it will be given to you" (Luke 6:38).* And as we have seen, Paul echoed the Lord in his second letter to the Corinthians: *"Whoever sows bountifully will also reap bountifully" (9:6).*

When we read these verses against the backdrop of an ancient Middle Eastern culture, they seem to make some dangerous promises. Namely, that material blessing is a sure sign of God's power and favor toward the giver, and the result of our sacrificial giving primes the pump of blessing. These verses seem to describe a *quid-pro-quo* between God and His people, a tit for tat regarding generosity and blessings. If we give to demonstrate our faith and trust, then He proves His trustworthiness by blessing us with health and wealth. We give, and then we get. Simple!

That is the basis of the so-called Prosperity Gospel. God has a storehouse of goods, and He is ready to pour it out—pour it back into our laps—if only we give.

The Prosperity Gospel says that when we do something by faith, the hand of God is moved to give us something in return. We give and then we get. We act, and then He acts. But trying to move the hand of God in our favor by what we do and say on earth is, well, pagan magic. That is what first-century Ephesians practiced, and what Paul warned against. At its core, the so-called Prosperity Gospel is nothing less than pagan idolatry and material wishes dressed in church clothes.

A CASE STUDY

Let me illustrate this point by relaying a story of a desperate businessman who came to me looking for a series of special prayers to move the hand of God in his favor.

One Sunday after our church worship service, I was greeting people, shaking hands, and thanking new visitors for attending. One man, about my age, was in the line, and seemed eager to speak with me. When he stepped up, he gave me his outstretched hand, shook firmly, and said that he would like to buy me a cup of coffee sometime during the week.

I seldom pass up an invitation like that, so I agreed. I asked him to call me and arrange a time and a date. He did so within a day, and later in the week, we met to talk. He told me a story about his struggling business and how I might help him out.

He seemed to be a great businessman. He had started, owned, and sold many businesses and franchise outlets over his years. He achieved a high level of success by his middle age. He attended church with his wife from time to time, but only for her sake. He was not a Christian believer. He didn't have the time or the interest to explore Christianity. He was often traveling or using Sunday as his only day to do what he wanted to do. It was his day off.

He was getting close to being able to retire, and his last business venture, he told me, was to purchase one last business that would pay him passive income over the rest of his life.

Then he got to the point. "David, I am a careful researcher of opportunities and the kind of businesses that can successfully exploit them. That is why I moved to Dallas. I knew that one of the most profitable businesses to own—one that would pay me repeatedly for the future—is an auto dent repair franchise. When it hails, people's cars get banged up. Car dealers can have hundreds of cars take a hit. The workers who fix these hail dents are hourly contract workers. They are well-paid, but they don't work directly for me. I don't have to carry them on my payroll. And the price I can charge to the car owner is always paid for by the insurance companies. And people around here have great insurance.

I was waiting for him to get to the point. He continued, "I did research on weather patterns all over the country. Historically speaking, the Dallas area gets walloped by hail at least every two years. Thousands of cars need repair. There is enough business in the Metroplex from one good hailstorm to keep me going for at least two years until the next major storm rolls in.

"So I bought a franchise here in North Dallas. In fact, I bought several of them. But, David, it hasn't hailed in this area in over five years. I do not have any business. I have had to put one of my franchises up for sale. I am losing my shirt on the others. I need it to hail."

At this point I started to suspect why he wanted to meet with me. So I asked him, "Are you asking me to pray for hail?"

He paused for a moment and, like a practiced businessman with a clear goal, he said, "Exactly! Will you? Will you pray for hail so I can get my company back on track?"

And then he added a bit of an incentive. "I know you are building an education wing for your congregation and that you need money. (We were building, and we always did need money, to be sure.) Here is my offer: if you will agree to pray for hail, and if it hails, I will give the church a significant contribution by the end of the first year."

He was growing desperate. He needed relief. In his mind, he needed a seasoned man of prayer to do (in effect) a rain dance—albeit for hail. It was the kind of request that wasn't different than the prayers and requests of millions of people everywhere, always, and in all places who desperately need God to act in their favor. "God, if you do for me, I'll do for you . . ."

Of course, I explained that prayer didn't work that way! I could not pray for the misfortune of others. I told him that I was not able to pray for money or incentives. But I did assure him that I would pray for him.

I also felt I had to address the incentive program he was offering me. I told him that my best advice for him was to investigate the claims of Christ as thoroughly as he investigated his business opportunities and to make God his partner in this venture and future ventures.

He was looking for magic. He had hoped that I could say some special prayers, induce a disastrous hailstorm, and save his plan for prosperity. He didn't believe in the Gospel, but he knew I did and he was trying to use my faith to increase his fortune and help me out at the same time.

NOT SO FAST

Like most false doctrines, the Prosperity Gospel grows from a kernel of truth. Indeed, God blesses those who generously give. Look again at Proverbs 11:25: *"A generous person will prosper; whoever refreshes others will be refreshed" (NIV).* Listen to Jesus' command to "*give, and it will be given*" (Luke 6:38). The Bible says that when we give, there is a return. However, God's blessings do not necessarily return to us in kind or on our schedule. Financial generosity does not guarantee a financial return. Nor does it usually come on the exact day we want it to come. Prayers, petitions, pledges, and payments do not provoke pennies from heaven, as it were.

Even Paul made this point. Read Paul's message to the Corinthians on this very subject.

> *He who supplies seed to the sower and bread for food will supply and multiply your seed for sowing and increase the harvest of your righteousness. You will be enriched in every way to be generous in every way,*

> *which through us will produce thanksgiving to God. (2 Cor. 9:10–11)*

Do you see it? Allow me to paraphrase. Paul said that God, who gives us the seed and the bread for food (thus everything), will multiply more seed. When we give seed (what God gives) and bread (what we make from it), it will produce more *seed* (not bread) and create a harvest of righteousness.

So to turn a phrase and make the point clearer, it seems that the Apostle Paul *did* believe in the Prosperity Gospel. Only he said it this way: when we give, it is the gospel that prospers!

Before we end this section, I must finish the story. I was not moved by his incentives to give the church money if my prayers worked. But I was moved by his boldness and courage. And yes, I prayed for him, for his business, and in the event of a hailstorm, for his prosperity.

BUT STILL THERE ARE TIMES

There is a real problem in speaking negatively about the way we give and the way God blesses us. To be critical of any connection between giving and receiving removes the love and the relationship between the giver and our God, who gives us all good things. Every person who has walked with God for any significant time can share a true story of His amazing provision. I certainly can. My wife and I have experienced outpourings of blessing after giving sacrificially to the work of building His

Kingdom. It happens. It has probably happened to you. When we give, we are blessed. Often. It doesn't happen all the time, but it happens enough to cause me to see a connection, and thank God every time for everything that I have received.

The key to unlocking this puzzle is to examine our motives. If we give to receive, we miss the point—and we will also miss the blessing. Perhaps this is the lesson for us as pastors. When we teach giving, generosity, and stewardship, we must stress the motives for giving and not the money we give. When we teach and preach stewardship, we must make it clear that the blessing of true discipleship, not of worldly riches, is the goal. Generosity doesn't get us the things we want unless what we want to be formed into the image of Christ.

MOVING ON

We have laid a foundation for stewardship and generosity based on the Bible's teaching, the local congregation's purpose, and the Apostle Paul's practices. There is so much more to say because, as we have seen, the Bible is chock-full of advice, counsel, teaching, preaching, examples, stories, warning, prophecies, parables, proverbs, and promises relating to money, stewardship, giving, offerings, generosity, and worship.

A field guide gives much more that the overviews we have seen so far. Let us move on to some common challenges and practical applications of stewardship and generosity.

5

TALKING ABOUT GENERATIONS

As this field guide gets further into areas of challenge and opportunity that we face along the journey, we should talk about one of the most amazing phenomena of the modern church. It is very multigenerational.

While individual congregations might be more "age and stage" churches, if we take Christianity as a whole, there has never been a more well-defined set of different generations alive at one time. In fact, for the first time in history, there are likely to be six or seven different generational groups in every church congregation.

When we talk about generosity—whether on Sunday morning or in a meeting of leaders—we perform a balancing act. On the one hand, we must present faithful theology and pastoral wisdom. On the other hand, we need to communicate practical lessons and doable steps. But each generation hears and sees things differently. One age group might be scandalized by the preachers' bold statements about the finances of the church. But another age group in the very next pew might say, "Finally, I am getting some authenticity here!"

As pastors burdened with the care of souls in our congregation, we need to offer the full breadth of biblical teaching on stewardship. But we must be wise in how we present it. We should consider our audience and how they will receive the message. People from various demographics, age groups, and experiences sit in our pews each week. Speaking to all these groups in a way that each of the groups can understand and appreciate is a tremendous challenge for the modern pastor.

Why? Because members of each generation prefer their own music, television shows, movies, hairstyles, language, phrases, sports and fashion icons, comfort food, and so on than other generations. When a person is born into this world and becomes an adult, both their peers' and parents' generation shape common attitudes and habits—particularly when it comes to giving. Knowing what each generation thinks about money better equips us to lead everyone into God's generous kingdom.

Adults in our congregations today fall into at least five groups: Generation Z, millennials, Generation X, boomers, and olders (the Silent and Greatest Generations combined because there are fewer of them). What must we do to engage such a broad mix of people? How can we activate a renewed vision of generosity when our audience ranges from early teen years to ninety or older?

Let's look at each generation, starting with the youngest.

GENERATION Z

Generation Z (born between 1997 and 2012) cares deeply for and collaborates with others. Self-driven and individualistic, they value flexibility and disdain traditional hierarchy of any type. They prefer to research a subject for themselves rather than be given a set of "facts." They want to reach their conclusions rather than join a bandwagon.

Texts, emails, FaceTime, direct messages, chatbots, dating apps, and all things virtual define the Gen Z world. They spend three hours a day on mobile devices!

Gen Zers tend to be pragmatic and authentic and value direct communications and personal involvement. Despite having all the latest technological gadgets at their fingertips, a recent Stanford University study reveals an intriguing twist: Gen Zers prefer face-to-face, one-on-one communications over all other forms. So, talk with them.

Don't expect Gen Zers to fill the old-school offering plate of their grandparent's generation. Seventy-five percent of this generation turn to Zelle or Venmo for money transfers. They bank with mobile apps. They don't write checks. They don't carry cash.

But this doesn't mean they don't have money. Generation Z cohorts invest online—most already own some form of stock, bonds, or savings tool. They fear accumulating debt that has hampered so many Gen Xers and millennials. They relish trust.

Gen Zers grew up in a time when everything happened at breakneck speeds; thus, they move fast but also want quality over quantity.

How do we reach Generation Z? *Invest* in them. They will be the future one day.

MILLENNIALS

Millennials (born between 1981 and 1996) grab most of the headlines today. They came of age in an online world of apps, social media, and video links. In 2020, according to the US Census Bureau, this cohort passed boomers to become the nation's numerically most significant living generation, with 72.1 million members.

While millennials outnumber other generations, they have fewer available financial resources than boomers or Gen Xers—at least right now. Many struggle with college debt, underemployment, and bad spending habits. But just wait. Their financial stature will change.

Along with their slightly younger counterparts in Generation Z, this cohort can expect to inherit more than thirty to $68 trillion. TRILLION is not a typo.

That is what Forbes magazine estimated in a November 2021 article. [2]

That is a lot of money. Yet if we pass an offering plate down a pew full of millennials, they might snap a picture and post it on Twitter or Instagram (#BrassPlate), but generally speaking, they will not put much of anything in it.

Why?

Are millennials simply self-obsessed or stingy? No. Let's not dismiss them that easily. Rather, let's look closer.

Millennials value support over subsidy. They want to be involved in the work they give to. Contrast this with boomers who tend to trust the institutions and missions they inherited from their parents. Moreover, boomers like me opt to believe that people can be deputized or appointed to represent the interests of a larger group, such as a church. While we boomers believe in an arms-length-away representative government, millennials believe in a participatory government.

How can we reach millennials? *Involve* them.

GEN XERS

Generation X (born between 1965 and 1980) represents about 20 percent of the giving population that lives in

---

2. Hall, Mark, (November 11, 2019) The Greatest Wealth Transfer In History: What's Happening And What Are The Implications accessed July 31, 2022 through Forbes.com

the United States. They make up about 25 percent of the entire population. People in this generation are more established and can give more significant amounts to churches and causes. The distinguishing mark of Generation X is their desire for results.

Gen Xers expect a bang for every buck they donate. They require facts and transparent accounting. They came of age during the information boom, the birth of social media, and the growth of mobile computing. They ask themselves, *Where will my money go, and what will it do for the cause I support?* If a Gen Xer passionately gives to a ministry or group, then that group is likely telling its supporters exactly what the donations accomplish.

Like millennials, this group is not known for supporting big or traditional institutions. They will support a ministry. But they want to know how it is making a difference.

Many Gen Xers have children who might benefit from Sunday school programs, vacation Bible schools, or youth ministries. But we cannot assume they will run to what we offer. We might have to stand in line behind other activities and opportunities such as sports, music camps, or science camps. Gen Xers value a "work-life balance." There are fewer workaholics and more hikers, bicyclists, and museum visitors.

Will Gen Xers give? Yes, of course! But this demographic will ask for some accountability and proven results for what they give. How do we reach them? *Inform* them.

BOOMERS

Now for the most extraordinary generation ever—the boomers! (Just kidding. I am prejudiced because I am a boomer.)

Boomers (born between 1946 and 1964) might have an argument for being the greatest when it comes to stewardship. They punch above their weight by contributing about *43 percent* of all charitable donations, yet they make up only one-third of the population, according to generations.com.[3]

Boomers appear to read printed ministry updates. They quickly fill out pledge cards and make monthly commitments. Moreover, they will place a check or donation in the collection plate on Sunday morning (though online giving for all generations is rising, especially as a result of the pandemic).

Whether or not boomers give, in the end, depends on whether they believe that the cause they're giving to has a good chance of success. What they consider worthy is not the same "value" criteria of millennials.

Worthiness often comes from reputation, presentation, or tradition: organizational boards, hierarchies, and representative leadership comfort boomers. Every pastor sees this dynamic when a boomer joins a church committee and governing group.

---

3. Gwoke, Phil, "Four Generations for Charity: Who Really Gives a Buck", accessed July 31, 2022 through Generations.com

The boomer speaks the language of commercials and the corporate world. Talk repeatedly turns to defining a strategic purpose or organizational alignment. They want to see the big picture and a clear vision.

How do churches reach boomers? *Inspire* them.

THE OLDERS

Last, but in no way least, come the olders. This group includes members of the Silent Generation and the Greatest Generation.

The olders (born in 1945 or earlier) have a deeper understanding of stewardship. They tend to write and mail checks and send handwritten thank-you notes. When it comes to giving online or responding to an internet appeal, they usually need help.

At first glance, it may seem that they do not crave involvement or activity in the church, but let's not be fooled. Many seniors, sadly, live in isolation. Sometimes this is due to health problems. Other times, especially as they enter their eighties and nineties, they have lost many family members and friends—people with whom they once had fellowship. Now they live in isolation.

This generation might love to have much more fellowship than most. But often, a church is so focused on attracting young people that the olders feel ignored. In their younger years, they made a mark on the world. As seniors, they still seek to make a difference, somehow and somewhere. They long to feel valued. Sometimes that happens with a simple hello.

Given their unfamiliarity with the digital world, many seniors only check their email about once a day, if that. By contrast, they relish a visit, letter, or phone call. Those who have the resources welcome appeals to give too. When they contribute financially, it helps them feel relevant and connected.

How are churches, then, to reach them? *Include* them.

SUMMARY

When it comes to Generation Z, we need to *invest* in them. Let them see the value of and result of their generosity. But also be transparent when something doesn't go according to plans. *Involve* millennials in the transformative aspects of giving. Let them see and feel how their giving helps others. For the Gen Xers, *inform* them how their donations make a concrete, real-world impact. Boomers are ready and eager to get involved. Someone needs to *inspire* them with a worthy cause or vision to work toward. Finally, the olders sincerely want others to *include* them in the giving process so they can feel the value of what they have to offer.

Just when we thought we had the unique aspects of each generation figured out, along comes the next generation. That would be Generation Alpha (born from 2013 until sociologists decide it is time for another shift). Generation A's oldest members will soon become teenagers, ready to handle rudimentary finances, old enough to comprehend and participate in stewardship. In reality—and biblically speaking—no age is too young to start a giving lifestyle. The seeds planted in childhood and teenage years will grow and bear fruit in adulthood.

Whatever generational differences, remember: a truly generous heart is moved by and dedicated to love for God and neighbor. No matter a person's age and approach, we must always appeal to giving with a spirit that embodies Christ and His Kingdom.

We may give in different ways, but we always give with a shared calling—to advance God's purpose for His creation and to share the love that guides and unites the whole body of Christ.

6

PREACHING STEWARDSHIP

After the discussion about the generations and their high-tech tools, social media, and mobile computing, it is time to mention the very old-school practice for which all of us were trained: preaching. As I believe we would all attest, there is no more important contribution that a pastor or priest or minister can make than to preach the Word of God rightly and duly administer the sacraments. As pastors we know this. Most of us treat preaching as a solemn obligation that requires study, prayer, preparation, practice, courage, and humility.

Thus, this field guide should include a lengthy chapter on the most important and widespread function that every Christian leader is trained to do: preach.

The pulpit is one of the key tools of proclaiming the Good News of Jesus Christ and His call upon us to be stewards of our life, time, and our gifts and resources.

But sometimes the message from the pulpit is not the "certain trumpet" that it needs to be, especially on this topic that everyone needs to hear. Let's look at a few reasons why this might be true in your context before we get to some specifics about preaching stewardship.

AN UNCERTAIN TRUMPET

I consulted with a leader and his vestry team a few years back. Their attendance was growing, but not their church finances. They had significant ministry opportunities but not enough money. This is not uncommon. Money follows ministry, but it often lags behind a year or two.

The senior pastor and the lay leadership team asked me to join them at their annual planning retreat to address the issue. After a long discussion, we devised a multi-year strategy to address the challenge of stewardship in the congregation. Of course, the centerpiece of the plan was the pastor's preaching on financial stewardship and biblical generosity.

All the leaders jumped on board the prayerfully considered game plan. Everyone seemed excited—except for the senior pastor. This young man's enthusiasm for teaching about money could best be described as tepid. That was a big problem. Shifting church-wide priorities toward healthy giving would not and could not happen without him.

We took a break after a late session, and, as the group disbursed for refreshments and restroom breaks, the pastor approached me. He admitted his reluctance at a very personal level. "These are great ideas, and the church should do them. And I know that doing so will require my strong commitment and participation. But I can't."

He had my full attention. His eyes moistened as he stared down to the floor. He continued, "My finances are a mess. I am drowning in debt because of bad choices my wife and I made a few years ago. I can't afford to give anything to the church. So far, I have avoided preaching about stewardship because I don't want to be a hypocrite asking others to do what I can't."

When he finished his confession, my heart went out to him. He was earnest and honest, but he felt he was unable to lead with an emphasis on sacrificial giving. I told him my story about being converted to the good news about giving that I related in the first chapter on this book. I encouraged him to resume regular financial giving, regardless of how small the amount. I was confident that, with the Lord as his helper, he would bring his family back from the brink of ruin to the joy of giving. While he and his family might feel material discomfort in the short term, the congregation and his personal spiritual life needed him to lead in faith and faithfulness.

WHAT IS YOUR "STEWARDSHIP STORY"?

Each of us has a unique history and perspective regarding personal financial stewardship. Like the sad scene noted above, I often hear pastors say that they cannot teach because of a sense of shame. Perhaps you feel this way too. You might believe that you have no right to teach others about a discipline you struggle to master in your own life. Fair enough. Fear not; many leaders carry baggage into the pulpit. If you have issues about past money mistakes, yes, you need to confess them, seeking healing and growth.

Every person has very real feelings about money and their finances. I have come to see that my reluctance in preaching the topic of stewardship in the early days of our church plant had to do with the struggles of my family of origin. My mother was a single mom with two young children in the late 1950s. She was alone in a very small town in Southern Arizona with no prospects for a career or full employment. I have clear memories from my childhood about her constant worry and tears over money, bills, and late payments.

When she married my stepfather, I am sure she thought her worries had come to an end—he was a well-known contractor with a nice new truck. But as it turned out, he also had a raging problem with alcohol. My mother's worries never stopped. And for most of my teenage years, she scrambled to make ends meet and to supplement my stepfather's income.

One Sunday she dragged my sister and me to church. It was a foreign atmosphere and experience to me. I do not remember much. But I remember her giving me a neatly folded-over check to put into the offering plate when it came. When she wasn't looking, I peeked at the inside of the check and read the amount. She gave an offering of four dollars. It was meager because her faith was meager, and her fear of poverty was great.

As I mentioned earlier, when I first considered preaching and teaching about stewardship, I knew that this memory and our family fear was behind my personal reluctance. I knew that if I preached on giving, I would have to lead in giving.

Today, the fact that we have given boldly and generously to our church—even a full tithe of our income—is a testimony to the power of God to change the human heart, my heart.

Whatever the reason for your silence or your slow-motion leadership on financial stewardship, you know what you must do. We all do. We all need to come to a point of trust and confidence like the Apostle Paul in prison. Remember that he learned the secret of being content in any and every situation because, as he so famously wrote, he could do all things through Him who gives us strength. Learning and growing alongside your parishioners can be incredibly powerful for them and you. Gen Zers, particularly, will love authentic transparency of your testimony and leadership.

BEST STEWARDSHIP PRACTICES

Throughout the years, I have delivered hundreds of sermons on generosity. I have also reviewed and critiqued (by invitation) other preachers' messages. While we each need to find our comfort level and voice, many best practices have emerged. These simple blueprints can turn what may seem like a treacherous task of preaching into a season of transformation.

Connect it to the biblical narrative. As we have seen, the stewardship themes run throughout the entire biblical narrative. In fact, in the ancient story of our beginnings, God gave Adam and Eve tasks: to work and keep a garden (see Gen. 2:15). They were responsible for its care. They were caretakers. Or to use a more biblical term, they were stewards. We know how the story turned out. The first couple blew it, and God banished them from Eden. But He didn't fire them!

If we read the story's text closely, Adam and Eve's physical location changed, but their primary job stayed the same. They still were called to be stewards; it just became more difficult.

Stewardship was the "job description" of our first parents, and it is still the same for all of humanity. We are all called to be stewards of the time, resources, gifts and talents, opportunities, and lifespans that each of us are given by God.

Again, if we read the text closely, we discover that in their fallen state, their assigned joint tasks for these two created images of God—both the male and the female—remained the same. Adam, and his helper and companion, Eve, were still required to tend the garden. Their tasks just became much more difficult. In

Genesis 3:17–19 God told Adam to toil over the ground for food.

To work and keep, i.e. stewardship, is the overarching Biblical trajectory where the narrative ends in another garden and a new city with a new Adam and Eve as the new bride (see Rev. 21–22). From the first garden to the last city, the biblical story is a tale of toil, trials, errors, efforts, accomplishments, advances, abdications, hopes, and disappointments by various people—finally culminating in the perfect work of Jesus Christ.

It is not too strong to say that the subtext for the entire biblical narrative is stewardship. So then whichever text we preach, we find the call to faithful stewardship. Once we see this common theme, we see it everywhere. In sermons and teaching, we must help our people see the link between everything they do in life and family and the great themes of stewardship and faithfulness to God—the task and toil of living an everyday, faithful life—under the Lordship of our Savior.

Emphasizing the biblical stewardship connection in our preaching allows us to see something that should *not* be the focus of our preaching: the church's budget and the fiscal needs facing the church. That is the last thing our sermons need to be about. The proper focus for all preaching—and for preaching about stewardship and generosity in particular—is not financial need but faithful stewardship.

Stay on target about treasure. As pastors and leaders, it is our nature to do just about anything we can to avoid the subject of money. We even go on long rabbit trails and sideways stories hoping that people will "catch on." In short, in our effort to nuance the subject of stewardship, we add other issues.

For example, when it comes to teaching on stewardship, we often roll out the "time, talent, and treasure" trope. We all know how it goes. We nudge people to contribute a few volunteer hours, some of their skills (time and talent), and bit of their money. In this equation—time, talent, and treasure (it comes so easily off the tongue), financial giving is downplayed. Inadvertently, time and talent gain a prominence, even to the point of substituting for financial generosity. Of course, a church needs hands-on work from its members. That might be an excellent way to build a new playground.

But the truth is that our churches typically spend forty-eight weeks a year recruiting and enlisting people for their time and talent. So four Sundays a year—one month—is not too much. When the time or season comes to talk about money, talk about money. Do not dilute the sacrificial nature of financial stewardship. Be focused. Be clear.

Take a cue from the Apostle Paul. He called the Corinthian Christians into a focused, deliberative process of deciding the amount of money to give to meet the needs of the Judean Christians. He did not ask them to volunteer their time or talents. Those may have been needed as well, but he didn't muddy the waters. Money was the most-pressing need, so he focused on that. No one in the Corinthian church would have been mistaken about his message.

Share real stories. As preachers, we hope our finely tuned theological expositions (sermons) will stir hearts and minds. While our doctrine must be correct, humans are hardwired to respond to stories. Most often, it is authentic personal testimonies that move people as well as good preaching. We need more of both.

People in the pews expect fervency and faith about generosity from their pastor. That doesn't surprise anyone. However, members of the church perk up when they hear stories from their peers in the pews about financial struggles, commitments, and blessings. That is powerful stuff. People can envision one person's generosity and how it might impact their own giving.

How do we find someone willing to tell their story about giving? Every believer has a testimony and most everyone is willing to share it when asked. Invite a few parishioners to share their stories. They should represent a cross-section of the congregation (married, single, young, old, rich, poor, white, black, Hispanic, Asian, etc.) so everyone can see a reflection of themselves.

I find it is helpful to meet with the people who will share during a live service. But it is even more important to meet with them ahead of time. Many people who think they are good at "winging it" often are not. Every pastor knows that from previous attempts to have people share. When I was in the pulpit, I would often interrupt my own sermon and invite a member to come up to the front where I could interview them with a few questions shared with them in advance. Or consider securing permission in advance and simply tell their story.

No matter how we go about sharing a personal story—live, interview, or video—people from the pews can effectively get a stewardship message to the people in the pews.

Tell it slant. There is a recipe for an effective sermon. Every pastor knows it. It involves sound biblical exposition and teaching, plus a powerful story of personal application or drama, and often a humorous anecdote or story. If our sermons have these three elements, we are well on our way to engaging the congregation.

What is the right balance? Emily Dickinson helps us. In her poem "Tell All the Truth but Tell It Slant," she captures it this way:

> *Tell all the Truth but tell it slant —*
> *Success in Circuit lies*
> *Too bright for our infirm Delight*
> *The Truth's superb surprise*
> *As Lightning to the Children eased*
> *With explanation kind*
> *The Truth must dazzle gradually*
> *Or every man be blind —*

As any effective public speaker knows, humor puts people at ease, especially when discussing a sensitive subject such as money. Repartee, especially laced with humor or wit, lowers defenses and opens hearts. That is what the poet means by "slant." She means to tell the truth, but help people see it coming out of the corner of their eyes before it stares at them right in the face.

Jesus used parables, analogies, metaphors, and narrative surprises to gently unpack truths that would otherwise be too dazzling or daring to comprehend. He told the whole truth and nothing but the truth, but to make His message accessible to regular people, He told it slant.

Consider, for example, Jesus' indirect, circuitous warning:

> *Do not lay up for yourselves treasures on earth, where moth and rust destroy and where thieves break in and steal, but lay up for yourselves treasures in heaven, where neither moth nor rust destroys and where thieves do not break in and steal. For where your treasure is, there your heart will be also. (Matt. 6:19–21)*

As a thought exercise, step back from the familiarity of this passage and read it with fresh eyes. Sure, it is not a riddle in the way we think of riddles today. It is not funny, per se. But in this passage, our Lord unfolds a profound and consequential truth. He tells us to be attentive to what matters most, which too often differs from what we pay attention to. But Jesus teaches in an almost absurdly earthy way. We are dazzled. We are charmed—and then His point sneaks up on us and grabs our hearts.

This is slant.

Find ways to follow our Lord's example when it comes time to preach about stewardship. Tell an embarrassing money story about yourself. Use surprising word pictures. Juxtapose seemingly opposite ideas. Tell a joke that sets people at ease.

Tell it slant.

Train stewards. Preaching is God's Word proclaimed, not a church budget itemized. There is a time and a place for comprehensive financial disclosure, but a sermon is not it. As excited as we are about what the church could do if people give generously, the preacher is not a pitchman. Furthermore, as important as transparency is, sharing a list of projects and programs is not appropriate from the pulpit. Save the program details and descriptions of financial needs for another time. Why?

When preaching is a sales pitch, the church becomes a product, and the authority of the preacher's voice is lost to a commercial.

I sold real estate for a few years before I went to seminary, and I did well. I found that I had a knack for communicating to my clients the benefits of specific homes and neighborhoods. That knack paid off. I was able to pay for seminary from the commissions I had earned.

Years later, as a young church planter, sometimes I slipped into a sales mode, leaning into the same instinct I depended on to be a successful realtor. It did not pay off in the pulpit! Why?

The church is not a consumer good. Listeners are not potential customers. Members are not clients. Instead, the church is an assembly of the saints. Parishioners are the body of Christ with hearts and souls. And my vocation is to proclaim Christ in Word and sacrament.

When we preach stewardship, our focus cannot be on raising money. Instead, we should train and raise stewards of life and life's resources. We must invite our listeners to encounter a faithful God afresh, and then respond in faithfulness with the finances He has entrusted to them.

And let's be gentle as we go. This is a significant paradigm shift for most people today.

Have a comprehensive annual plan. To have practical training on financial stewardship, the pastor should have a comprehensive, church-wide, communication plan, not just a few sermons in a series. In addition to preaching about offerings from the pulpit, you should consider what additional resources, workshops, classes, or groups your people need to help them internalize and practice the spiritual discipline of generosity.

I cannot presume to instruct you or your church leadership about how to launch a full campaign for stewardship education that reaches every member of your church. I cannot know what a program would look like in your context. But you do! You know how your people think, how they receive information, what leaders need to be involved, who needs to be contacted or visited, and what staff or lay leaders need to be recruited, organized, and empowered. You know all of that.

In this chapter, I am trying to convey a simple idea. Your pulpit is a key ingredient—I would even say a central part of leading your church to understand, apply, and grow as a faithful community of responsible stewards. Do not neglect the duty to preach the good news of giving.

If you have any doubt about the elements of a stewardship program in your church, enlist Google to help you see what other congregations are doing. It is not rocket science. But in the end, you will probably find that you must work with your ministry staff and lay leaders to prepare logistics, materials, schedules, and personnel. You're aiming for sustained, cohesive messaging across all your ministries and departments. Everybody needs to get in on the stewardship action, including youth, children, and seniors.

The goal is a whole, healthy church full of faithful stewards from top to bottom.

7
DEVELOPING STEWARDS IN THE CHURCH

For some leaders, speaking publicly about stewardship is the easiest part. Most pastors love to preach. But fewer, by far, enjoy the next step: having face-to-face conversations with church members to have heart-to-heart conversations about their financial support of the church. But a church must develop regular, dedicated generous donors committed to the mission of the congregation. Nurturing these people often requires a personal touch. The next few chapters of this field guide will open this subject and give tools and words for the pastor's work.

Talking about money does not have to be a favorite thing for pastors to do. But it does have to be a regular thing—a routine part of the way a pastor leads the congregation. Over time, we can even become good at it—or at least more comfortable. I didn't like the assignment at first. But over time, I began to cherish the personal, pastoral interactions with people about their love and support for the church.

To best equip pastors from a wide range of churches and denominations to have these conversations, please allow me to share everything I know about doing it wisely and pastorally. My comments here come from three decades of personal experience and from others I have counseled. I was the founding pastor of the church where I spent the subsequent thirty-one years. I know that this was a privileged position; it gave me huge credibility among our members. But as I have consulted with other pastors, I have seen other leaders walk faithfully in this area and walk boldly in drastically different situations. I can draw on their experience as well.

So here is what I know.

Put very simply, the lead pastor should ask staff and lay leaders to develop the expense side of an annual budget. Both annual and capital budgets are developed differently in different traditions and congregations, and a wise pastor is always involved in the process. Out of necessity, other leaders and staff can be deputized to develop a financial spending plan for the church. Of course, the senior pastor has a say and sway over the final budget, but the financial details (expense allocations, etc.) are often best determined by the people closest to the ministry program.

However, responsibility for developing the income side of an annual or capital budget rests with the senior pastor. If, as I proposed earlier this book, financial stewardship and generosity are spiritual issues central to the life of a disciple of Christ, they fall under the purview of the senior leader's ministry mandate. It might be tempting to delegate these money matters to other leaders, but lead pastors must pray long and hard before handing off these essentials to someone else. Why?

If the senior pastor is both the leader of the vision and the spiritual development for the congregation, then *only* the senior pastor should make personal visits to donors and other leaders to help underwrite the budget and the program of the congregation. Who else can sit in the home of members and ask them to give generously of their money for the ministry of the church? In most denominations and Christian traditions, the senior pastor must learn how to talk to donors and leaders about their financial involvement in the church.

This is not easy for pastors. Talking with members about their support is not our first language. We can sit with members and ask them to become more involved in the life and ministry of the church. We know how to recruit leaders and volunteers. But when it comes to stewardship and generosity, many pastors freeze. We often do not know what to do. We don't know what to say.

In the rest of this chapter, I will outline a method of visitation and conversation with donors in the congregation that I have found to be pastorally sensitive and useful.

Please read through this section to the end. I want to be sure that those who read this chapter will also know that I do not consider these efforts as primarily fundraising. These visits are intended to help members ask and answer a crucial question that should answered by every disciple: *What does God want to me to do with the resources entrusted to me to support the ministry of my church?* That is not a financial matter; it is a pastoral one.

Here are the elements of such a conversation.

MAKE A LIST

Make a list of the 5–20 percent (or so) members and donors who are committed to the church by giving their time, talent, and financial resources. This list should be made up of the most committed core people in the church.

I am not referring only to those who give the most. Of course, they should be on this list. But we should only include them if there are other indicators of their commitment and love for the church. As pastors, we are not engaged in the work of developing wealthy philanthropists. The donors we want to develop already love the church. They consider the church their home congregation. They have a strong affection for and trust in the pastoral leadership. They have fellowship with other members. They believe in the mission and feel a personal stake in the congregation's progress toward realizing the mission.

Most of the people on our list should come quickly to mind, but other staff and lay leaders can make sure that no one is left off. Development of this list is a very important part of the process.

PREPARE IN HEART AND PRAYER

Once we have the list together, the next step is to prepare for a personal visit. Asking for people's financial support is most effective when done face-to-face and heart-to-heart. These precious people are part of Christ's flock, and as pastors, we are their under-shepherds. Their spiritual life and health must always be our priority, not solely their ability to give.

As we prepare to meet with individual church members, we should pray specifically about the task. When I have done this in the past, I have prayed in advance that my heart be filled with humility before God and love for His people. I ask for supernatural levels of courage, wisdom, and reliance on God's Spirit. I also pray for God to prepare people's hearts and minds long before the actual conversation starts. In my personal prayers, I ask that these conversations catalyze a more profound longing for God in their lives and mine.

A RIGHT ATTITUDE

This bears repeating: pastorally speaking, our goal is not to raise money but to raise faithful stewards. Remember, a church's financial needs are not equally divisible by the number of members. Believing that two hundred families can best meet a $400,000 budget by each giving $2,000 assumes that each family has equal financial resources and priorities. This also assumes that every family will give, and $2,000 is the most that anyone should give. These are not safe assumptions. Equal membership fees by each family happens at a country club, rotary club, or homeowner's association. Not the church. Let's not treat the finances like we are handing members a bill.

Regardless of age, income, family status, or other demographic factors, every person in our church can become a generous giver. But generous doesn't mean equal in amount. Faithfulness and generosity are expressed differently according to each person's or family's circumstances. Remember Paul's admonitions to the Christians in Corinth? *"If the readiness is there, [a financial gift] is acceptable according to what a person has, not according to what he does not have"* (2 Cor. 8:12). Giving must be in keeping with a family's financial ability and obedience to the Spirit's prompting, not according to the church's needs.

PREPARING TO VISIT

We have made a list of prospective donors. We have prayed. Now we need to ask to meet with an individual or family to talk about their financial support.

Let's start with some nuts and bolts. We should make an in-person meeting request through a generationally and culturally appropriate medium. A boomer will pick up the telephone and make a call. A Gen X leader might prefer email. A millennial will probably gravitate toward text messages. Before we call, send, or text, let's flip the perspective. What will the recipient feel most comfortable with? We should consider each person, couple, and family separately—but as a general rule, I use snail mail for anyone older than forty-five and text messages for anyone thirty-five and younger. The squishy middle's preferences will vary from person to person.

What we write and our tone can make a huge difference. There should be no room for ambiguity in the request for a face-to-face meeting. We are not asking for five minutes after church. Nor do we want to send them a form letter. We are not asking them to attend a seminar. Nor are we asking for a check or financial gift. We want to meet. We want to talk.

We are their pastor now and still want to be their pastor in the future. We cannot sacrifice a long-term relationship to fulfill a financial need in the short-term.

Unless we pastor a very large church, we likely have a prior relationship with the person or family we will meet with. It bears repeating: first and foremost, we are their pastor. In setting up a meeting with them, we should communicate the purpose of the meeting. In other words, there should be no surprise as to the intent of the meeting. This is not bait-and-switch.

Here is the relevant part of a letter I wrote a few years ago.

> *Dear Joe and Judy,*
>
> *I am writing to ask for a few minutes of your time. As you know, our church is in the middle of an exciting stewardship teaching program. As part of the program, I am having conversations with a few members about where we are going as a community of faith. We have great opportunities ahead and still we face certain financial realities. In our time together, I would like to share these—the opportunities and the realities—with you.*
>
> *I would love to come over to visit in the next week. May I call you in the next few days to find the time for the three of us to meet? If you want to text me a time that you'd be available, please use this number: 555-280-2233. That is my cell number and of course, you can always call me.*

This letter should be brief. And to underscore the point made above, the letter is from a pastor to members of the congregation. It is built upon relationships. There should be no hint of pressure in asking for a visit. Instead, because of our personal and pastoral relationship, there is a high likelihood that the individual or family will agree to set up a time for the meeting.

There are a few helpful things we should remember when setting up an appointment:

- Be sure that (if the member is married) both the husband and the wife will be present for the appointment.
- Suggest meeting in their home and at their convenience. Some members prefer to go to a coffee shop or have lunch together. In a few situations, members can be invited to come to the pastor's office.
- I prefer that the specifics on the meeting should be made in writing and mailed with a stamp. This sets a serious and respectful tone.
- A few days after the letter should have arrived, make a phone to confirm a time and location. While an administrative assistant can make this call, I suggest it come from the pastor to keep the entire exchange personal.

A SAMPLE CONVERSATION

When we can meet with the individual or couple, we need to bring up the purpose of the meeting and subsequently ask for a financial commitment. This is why we are there face-to-face, and it is up to us to bring the subject up.

However, before I share a sample conversation, allow me to make a few observations about what can be said and how it can be said. Again, I hesitate to do this because every conversation I have ever had about giving has been couched in the language of brotherly love and pastoral care. But I do want to point out a few characteristics about how I have handled these meetings:

- I will not push an individual or couple to decide about giving on the spot. I will ask them to pray about deciding.
- I couch the entire request in terms of the congregation's vision and the mission that God has set before the church.
- I am quiet once the request is made. When I ask the question, I remain silent until they give their answer.
- After an answer is given, I thank the couple for their faithfulness and support, and I leave shortly after that.

Here is a presentation that can be made to a couple in their living room.

> *Tim and Carol, I want to thank you for the time to meet today. I have a request to make of you, but I want to back up and ask you to think about where we*

are as a parish. [Here, I outline the specific intention of our effort. It could be to raise money for an annual budget, a capital expense, or a needed mission project.]

I have been out visiting people in our church to ask for their help. You know that we need to do this, and I believe that we can do it. But to get there, I need your help. We need to raise _____ dollars to get our project underway. And, as you know, that is a lot for our church. People are excited about it. I know I am. But many people in our congregation believe that our program is out of reach for us. I don't think it is. But this is where I need your help. Our church needs a few families to step up and make larger-than-normal financial commitments to this project. And frankly, I am asking if you can do that.

We know that we can't ask every family in our church to give the same amount. It doesn't work that way. But I am asking you—along with a few other families— to lead the way for our church. This would create extraordinary momentum and help us get where we need to be. So, I am asking you to consider this. Would you be willing to pray about the possibility of giving a leadership gift of _____ to our church for the project?

At this point, it is best to be quiet and let the specific prayer request settle in. I am not asking for a yes or no answer for a specific amount, only that they pray about it. I have asked the individual or couple to pray about giving at a specific level. I have asked the question with grace and confidence, and I have invited them to begin a journey of discovering how best they can answer the call upon their lives to be generous stewards.

Most couples readily agree to pray about my request—which is a request for them to pray. And honestly, that is all I am asking them to do.

Depending on the type of campaign or the need for the funding, there are myriad ways to express a request. Here are a few sentences or phrases that you might find useful, depending on your circumstances.

FOR AN ANNUAL BUDGET CAMPAIGN

I am excited to see our church's momentum as we complete this year and prepare for next year. I am asking twenty families to pray about increasing their church giving by 20 percent for next year. Would you be willing to pray about being one of those families and increasing your giving?

FOR A SPECIAL MISSION PROJECT

We have an opportunity to send a mission team overseas this year. We have some funds already set aside for this, but we need a few more sponsors willing to give $2,000 more than their normal giving. I am asking five families in the church to pray about this. Would you be willing to pray about becoming one of those sponsoring families?

FOR A LARGE PURCHASE NEEDED FOR MINISTRY

We have determined that we need to make this purchase happen. We have some of the money in our budget, but we don't have it all. We need an additional $25,000 by the end of the summer. Will you be willing to pray about making a major gift toward that need?

ANOTHER APPROACH

Each of us has a unique relationship with each member of the church. I would never recommend that you use my exact words to ask your members for greater financial generosity. The words you use should be the words that are natural and personal to you in your own setting.

As a way to provide an additional example, I have asked a good friend and expert in the field of church fundraising to offer his own words. For many years, Ben Gill served as president of Resources Services, Incorporated, and he is a friend. Ben was first a pastor and then a professional capital campaign consultant.

Here is Ben's input:

Situation: The pastor is a close friend to the potential donors, Tim and Carol Smith. Tim and Carol have been leaders in the church for more than thirty years. They are committed stewards. The pastor is meeting them in their home. He will be asking them to consider a lead gift of $500,000. The total project cost is $5 million for a new sanctuary.

The pastor transitions the conversation to the purpose of his visit.

> *Carol, Tim was telling me the other day that you have never been in a church where a totally new sanctuary was built. Well, neither have I. Every church I have worshiped in was paid for and built by someone else. And now, it is our time. It is our time to build a place of worship. I sense that you feel that excitement too.*
>
> *Tim, Carol, I am taking some time this week to look for the lead gift in our stewardship campaign. When I made my list, your family was the first on it.*
>
> *That is why I am here tonight. I want to ask if you would pray about making the $500,000 lead gift toward building the new sanctuary?*

At this point the pastor should not say another word until they have given their answer.

Note: If they say yes, then give them a timetable.

> *We are trying to obtain the lead pledges and commitments by Monday of next week. Will you pray about it? I will be praying for you as you go through this decision process. Would you mind if I pray with you before I go?*

If they say no, then thank them for their time, pray with them, and leave. In thirty-five years of fundraising, I have never had anyone say they won't pray about the decision. Of course, people will pray!

These presentations show different ways to request participation in financial giving. Your words, in real time, will reflect your personality as well as the character of the relationship between you and the donor.

SUMMARY AND A FINAL POINT

The senior pastor is the one person most responsible for raising the resources for the congregation's mission. Personal heart-to-heart visits with members and potential donors can be one of the most effective ways of helping people know how to give wisely and prayerfully to support the congregation.

Some people suggest that gathering money for ministry should be easy. It is not. Finding donors who will give sacrificially to the vision and purpose of a congregation is hard work. People will spend blithely in token amounts for many things. But that is not what I mean by developing donors for ministry. Generally speaking, we develop sacrificial donors over years of relationship, trust, accountability, and honest and caring relationships.

One more final point. There is a myth to developing donors for ministry that can be personal for a pastor. If an individual or couple say no, we should not consider this a personal rejection. Never. If we have strong relationships with the people we are leading, we love them in the Lord. We care about their spiritual life more than their financial commitment to the church. If we ask them for greater financial support—then after prayer and consideration, they decline—we should not take their decision personally. They prayed and God answered their prayer.

8
ESTIMATE OF GIVING CARDS

Remember our friends at St. Archimedes? They do a lot of ministry and community outreach on a modest budget. The pastor teaches biblical generosity. Members embrace it. That's the big picture, but sometimes speed bumps come along the way that impede giving or make it uneven throughout the year.

When gas prices go up, the wallets of congregants empty faster. If ten members lose their jobs, the offerings might suffer. Some people in the church give when they attend, but only when they attend! Some members wait for the "Spirit to move" and give only a little.

Early on, the staff and elders at St. Archimedes realized that these scenarios and dozens more could derail the church's mission. How could they avoid a sudden shortfall?

St. Archimedes needed a clear-sighted gauge to estimate what funds might be received each month and for the year. Not just weekly tithes, but offerings too. Not the Christmas bonuses, but predictable donations. With written expectations in hand, they could create a budget.

Like many church committees, our friends turned to a written estimate of giving cards, or pledge cards, as a primary stewardship tool. These financial promise notes historically play a crucial role in church fundraising. So the move made sense.

How pledges work and why a ministry would want to use them may seem obvious, but stay with me. Like almost everything else we thought was acceptable in church ministry, a growing number of today's pastors view this promise-making system as outdated—from the days of the dinosaurs. Other leaders, including me, still see some benefits but also raise legitimate red flags.

What about pledge cards? What about "estimate of giving" cards? Are they useful? Desirable? Dependable? Should Christians be asked to sign an annual financial commitment to indicate what they intend to donate in a year or toward a specific capital project?

Henri Nouwen reminds us, *"Fundraising is proclaiming what we believe in such a way that we offer other people an opportunity to participate with us in our vision and mission."*

Pledge cards enable leaders to fulfill their vision and equip members to participate. Why? Because after pastors and finance committees have donation estimates, they can build better budgets for their capital campaigns, special projects, and operational expenses. They know what to expect.

As for donors, when they sit down to fill out an estimate of a pledge card, they do something meaningful. They first contemplate the need, reflect on their situation, collect the facts, and then pray. Individuals and couples examine their intentions. Why are they giving? Guilt? Peer pressure? Or God-directed, biblical, servant-heart-driven generosity? In a sense, pledge cards are intention cards. When a church member fills out and signs a pledge card, it is not a binding contract. Nor is the promised dollar figure owed to the church. It is a broad estimate from a dedicated member that expresses their intent to fulfill the amount.

Some churches have a long tradition of pledge cards. The leaders and the congregants cannot imagine not using them. These congregations make an annual effort to distribute pledge cards to and collect them from every household in the church. Committees then form the budget based on the totals pledged.

A few churches balk at the word "pledge" but need some budgetary mechanism. They tend to tweak and rename the process. Some hand out "estimate of giving" cards. These tools essentially serve the same purpose.

On the flip side, some congregations eschew pledge cards altogether. Instead, they take other means to educate their members, gather ballpark donation numbers, and collect offerings. These churches, like their pledge-based counterparts, fulfill their mission quite well. Usually, they do it on a balanced budget too.

Before we ponder the pros and cons of pledge cards, let's venture into the weeds of history. Stay with me. The Bible doesn't mandate that anyone provide a written estimate of donations. But it is not unbiblical, and the backstory to the pledge system is fascinating.

THE FASCINATING BACKSTORY OF A WRITTEN PLEDGE

As late as the fifteenth century, most church attendees stood for the entire length of a service. A few brought stools to sit on. Some churches scattered hard benches around the nave.

Can you image the disarray this setup created? Congregational leaders no doubt yearned for a more orderly appearance. As sermons grew longer, the clergy likely wanted a place for everyone to sit and vice versa and attendees surely pined for seats. As the sixteenth century approached, benches without wooden backs came into vogue. They were arranged in rows. This evolved to the point where well-financed congregations, starting in Europe, installed permanent pews complete with wooden backs. Finally, members could sit down during worship.

Wood and labor for these upgrades came with a price tag, of course. How could churches of that day acquire the needed funds? Creative leaders hatched a plan. They rented the new pews to attendees. Wealthy members snatched up most of the seats. Old wooden pews of this type still exist in a few historic churches in New England and Europe.

Once the initial construction costs were covered, churches continued to rent the pews to parishioners. They were hooked on the income stream. Soon enough the proceeds helped fund general operating expenses and other mission needs.

As the flow of money came in, rents skyrocketed in some churches. Others got creative. For example, for years (in the late 1700s) St. Mary's Church in Philadelphia auctioned their pew boxes to the highest bidder. Rents were collected on a quarterly basis, and fees were expensive. Annual rent at St. Mary's was about $100 per pew, which is about $3,500 dollars in today's currency! Pews in preferred spots commanded higher sums. Small, less desirable seats were located at the back of the sanctuary, not unlike coach seats in modern airlines.

Some parishes put out pew rental advertisements that read something like this:

> *All members of the parish should have their names entered into the Pew Rent Register. This rule includes single men and woman as well as the married. There are single sittings for the single wage-earner*

> *or salary-drawer. Per rent is to be paid quarterly in advance. Per holds requiring more time to pay their pew-rent should notify the pastor. . . . If anyone . . . cannot rent a sitting, let him inform the pastor and he shall have a sitting assigned to him and receive credit for full payment in the annual report. This is all we require of the poor.*

Most churches made provisions for every member of the congregation to have a place to sit for worship. Some pews were even fitted with coal-fired foot warmers. Some had personalized carvings or ornate decorations indicating the relative wealth of the renters. A few pews had small entry doors to keep out non-renters.

And the pews were numbered like the seats at a sports stadium.

THE ANNUAL PLEDGE

We are in the weeds, I know. But there is a point to be made here. This elaborate pew rental system was developed as a useful way to finance the church operations. It remained a widespread practice until after the Second World War. What replaced it? That's right: the annual pledge. How did parishioners make that pledge? They filled out and turned in cards that included their giving estimates.

By the time boomers came along, open seating was the norm, as it is today. That made for a more welcoming service but hurt the bottom line. Leaders of the day faced big questions. How can we pay for the operating expenses and upkeep of the congregation? How can we commit to our mission and fulfill our vision? How can we be confident there will be enough funds? These questions drove fundraising to the annual pledge system, which is much the same as pledge cards today.

Member families were canvassed every year and asked to sign a pledge card to indicate a financial amount for their support of the church. These families were then provided a box of envelopes (fifty-two for weekly tithes and a few more for special offerings and holidays). They were expected to use the envelopes to send the church the money they had pledged.

This is the history of annual pledges. As mentioned, using them is not a biblical mandate. The system was relatively short-lived, albeit intriguing. As can be inferred, the system was developed to solve a problem, not necessarily to teach and encourage biblical stewardship for the individual believer or couple.

BENEFITS OF PLEDGES

Does the pledge card simply trying to solve the same problem? Namely, to have an accurate financial forecast. Is it a means to a specific end—a balanced budget? Or does it clutter the biblical way of generosity? Does it mix motives or help focus the vision?

Some leaders say, "Yes. We want pledges." Others say, "Never!"

Let's look at the pros and cons of pledge cards as most often used today to help us navigate this dilemma. Here are four good reasons to consider using a pledge card system:

Pledges are a biblical practice. Please note that I am not saying that writing a pledge card is biblical. As we have seen, it is a modern practice. But the Bible fully supports the act of making a pledge, promising to give a certain amount of money.

This seems to be what Paul suggested in 2 Corinthians 8. It might be hard to see the apostle's point through the layers of history and ancient culture, but it does appear that the early church in Corinth and Macedonia made some sort of pledge or commitment. Paul wrote to the Christians in Corinth: *"And in this matter, I give my judgment: this benefits you, who a year ago started not only to do this work but also to desire to do it. So now finish doing it as well, so that your readiness in desiring it may be matched by your completing it out of what you have"* (2 Cor. 8:10–11).

Did they sign a pledge papyrus, rather than our sharply printed paper cards? We do not know if individual members of the congregation made specific promises, but part of the back story of 2 Corinthians 8–9 is that Paul encouraged the Corinthians to make a concrete, specific decision about giving. They had made their decision in good faith, and later Paul sent his assistant to encourage them to follow through with it.

Making a pledge fosters commitment. When a person signs a pledge card, he or she makes a powerful statement. It communicates commitment to the church. It is not a legally binding contract, to be sure. Most pledge cards contain a statement that allows for changes to be made in the pledge at any time. But there is an air of formality or seriousness.

Jesus said that wherever we put our treasure, we can find our hearts. By extension, we might hope that wherever we decide to put our treasure, our hearts will follow. Asking church attendees to step forward and sign a pledge card will engage them with a serious question: Are their hearts in it? They are invited to consider drawing nearer to the life of the church family. The commitment of signing a pledge card often helps people truly feel like this is their church.

Pledges empower leaders. As the leaders of the congregation wisely steward finances, what basis do they have for longer-term commitments? Can the church responsibly hire staff to serve without knowing the level of financial support? When should a building project be undertaken? Without a clear picture of the funds to be committed, how can the church know what is possible and responsible? A pledge system empowers the leadership by letting them know (with a certain amount of faith) what kind of financial base they can count on going forward.

Pledges can flag pastoral issues. The process of making a pledge and tracking its fulfillment creates a helpful feedback loop. If someone falls behind on their pledge, this should create a notification to the staff that can lead to a helpful pastoral conversation. Perhaps the family has experienced a job loss and needs pastoral care or financial support.

Maybe the person's faith has waned. Maybe someone needs to be encouraged to follow through on their commitment (as the Corinthians needed!). A person's priorities usually can be seen in their calendar and checkbook. The pledge system gives a window into someone's checkbook and financial life in a unique way that can flag needs or problems.

DRAWBACKS

Pastors and elders must consider one other factor. Some cast aspersions on the yearly pledge card system as "old school" in the sense that it could feel dated and stale. However, the most "old school" thing about the annual pledge card system in many churches is the "old school" assumption about income.

Put simply, the annual pledge card system assumes income stability and job continuity that no longer matches the reality in most of our ministry contexts. The annual pledge card system depends on each member having an accurate projection of his or her income for the next year—a projection that can be used as the basis for an annual budget.

Let's think about this with clear heads. Older members in our churches who belong to the Great and Silent generations likely worked thirty or forty years for the same company. They knew exactly how much they got paid each month. They could estimate reasonable raises. And they could at least pencil in bonuses. They could predict their personal financial flow, which enabled them to give accurate giving estimates.

How does this stack up against today's reality? How many of our church members work at commission-based jobs? What about those among us who work in the so-called gig economy? Gigs give people freedom with their time, and they can work multiple side hustles. But they never know what their income will be from week to week, let alone year to year.

A commission or gig worker can guess their income, but it will be a wild guess. In a pledge card system, if members meet their earning goals, then the church meets its budget. If not, everyone is in trouble.

Pledge card systems can be counterproductive in this regard. When someone fails to fulfill his or her pledge, a sense of guilt and obligation often follows. But we must preach grace and forgiveness, not establish systems that depress.

We want people to give generously, cheerfully, and sacrificially. The pledge card system can turn giving into just another bill to pay. Even if the person eventually fulfills his or her pledge, discipleship may have taken a back seat.

THROUGH A DIFFERENT LENS

As I write this chapter, I realize that too often we view the decision for or against a pledge card system from the church's perspective. What works best for our vision and mission? After all, churches use an annual pledge card system so we can accurately forecast income and budget expenses.

However, let's turn the tables and ask what would be best for the members of our congregation. With the pledge card system, members mainly focus on giving to during an annual drive. That's when they pray and make a commitment. The rest of the year, they give, but their attention drifts to other matters.

If stewardship holds a central part of God's discipleship plan for each Christian, would it be better to have a more holistic way? How can we have a comprehensive fundraising mechanism that not only brings in money but also helps our members discern or discover a way of being a faithful steward of what God has given them—all year long? Can we teach stewardship and raise good stewards in a more holistic way?

INHERENT CHALLENGES

Some people contend that any sort of "estimate of giving" card system is "old school." That in itself is not bad; being old does not discount it out of hand. Not at all. Many churches have used them for decades and will continue for the foreseeable future. However, there are some growing and serious drawbacks to an annual pledge-card approach. Let's look a bit closer at the inherent challenges of an exclusively pledge-based program.

First, a pledge-card system creates a dilemma. Much effort goes into helping people fulfill their pledges. Then what? For many people, if they have met their estimated donation goal, they rightly assume their giving for the year is done. This satisfaction of personal success comes based purely on a dollar figure target. Their giving may or may not have been sacrificial. It may or may not be commensurate with the person's or family's financial ability. None of those factors matters—the person has completed their pledge. Mark it PAID. Worse yet, if an urgent ministry need arises, a member who has fulfilled their pledge might conclude that they have done what was asked of them. In other words, the pledge card system can put an artificial ceiling on giving.

Second, as diligent as leaders can be in collecting pledges from church members, the total number of pledges returned never equals the number of individuals and couples who consider themselves part of the fellowship. Typically, an annual pledge card program only involves between 60 percent and 70 percent of regular attendees who turn in a signed pledge card. That means the ingathered pledges do not represent the whole church—one-third of the church has been non-committal.

When churches rely primarily or solely on the pledge card system through an annual appeal rather than ongoing attention to generosity, then the pledges become self-fulfilling prophecies. If only 70 percent of the church is pledging and the budget is built on only that pledged income, then the church is functioning at 70 percent of its potential.

Third, the church's finance committee often hesitates to budget more than the pledged amount. This produces an implicit signal that the church is settled, rather than growing. The church is relying on members giving year to year, rather than focusing on generosity that should be growing year by year—both among members and with new people. The pledge card system might communicate a settled status quo (like an insider club membership) rather than the growing momentum of a congregation participating in the mission of God and seeing people added to their number regularly.

The COVID-19 pandemic hit pledge-card-reliant churches hard. Many abandoned the practice. The shutdown caused church leaders to encourage their members to give by online means. Recurring, automatic giving has been a blessing to every congregation because it has assured a level of support from the families in a church regardless of weekly church attendance.

This auto-draft method might have thrown a life preserver to congregations during a pandemic, but wise leaders should know that it can easily erode people's spiritual and financial commitment to the vision and mission. When giving is done online, it is unseen. The church can become out of sight and out of mind. What kind of experience is giving freely and sacrificially if it is an Electronic

Funds Transfer (EFT)? Over the next few years, congregations should think deeply about ways to helping online givers give something during a worship service–even if it is only symbolic.

What would a holistic, comprehensive emphasis look like in the local church? What would it look like for a congregation to teach and train people in the generous ways of the Christian faith? Read on.

9

BUDGET BASICS AND YEAR-END GIVING

As pastors, we should teach and preach generosity to raise good stewards. When members of our congregations see their calling as caretakers of God's creation (toiling and tending), and then live out that call, our marketing programs to ramp up donations become moot. In an ideal world, stewards will grasp and embrace giving, the church's ministry thrives, and the gospel message flourishes.

Alas, we do not reside in a utopia. Life happens, and people's commitment to biblical stewardship frequently wanes. Newcomers arrive and have an old habit (or no habits) about giving. Others in our midst struggle with basic money principles—they struggle with income, expense, debt, or spending problems. We must constantly teach, train, and reinforce biblical generosity.

Still, this will rarely be enough. That is reality.

In reality, many leaders see their congregation's giving fall short of what was pledged. Most churches run low on or out of funds by Christmas—sometimes by Thanksgiving. A gentle reminder nudges a few members to catch up on their pledge-card promises. Others need stronger, personal appeals. If the nudges and appeals work, giving might double in the last month of the year. (Indeed, most churches find that their income comes into the church over twelve full months—but December offerings often double.)

Before we dig into ways we can handle a year-end cash flow crunch, let's get on the same page regarding the technical elements of a church's budget challenges.

THE FOUR *B*'S OF THE BUDGET

Some senior pastors take a hands-off approach to the financial realities of their congregation. I have seen this often in the clergy I have consulted or coached. They do not know the basic facts about the church's budget or weekly offerings. They do not know how much debt the church is carrying. They tell me rather glibly that they have a finance committee that minds everything.

I cannot understand this willful ignorance of something as vital as the financial health of their congregation.

Of course, money is not the most important thing. We all agree on that. It is not front and center in the congregation's mission—unless you run out. When a church runs out of money, that is all the members think about. It is the number one topic of conversation during coffee hour and the subtext of the "ministry updates" and "staff change" announcements on Sunday. And when the church runs out of money—or runs too close to the bone to do its mission—most people look to the senior pastor and ask, "Why? What happened?" As well they should. The senior pastor should be the most well-informed person in the church about the health of the congregation's income and outflow.

I am constantly amazed by the number of pastors I speak with who shrug their shoulders. They do not know these basics about their church. Any serious potential donor should have second thoughts about investing in a mission where the senior leader is clueless on money matters.

As noted earlier, for myriad reasons, the pastor must know their church's specific financial facts and health. They do not need a degree in accounting to run the ministry, but pastors should be current on a few key details. It is not complicated. It does not require advanced learning. There are a few critical areas of church finances that the senior pastor, as we say in the old Anglican collect, must "read, mark, learn, and inwardly digest."

For those not inclined to know financial things, there are only four numbers that the senior pastor needs to know—at a minimum.

- *The Budget.* How much money does the church need on an annual basis? What is the total budget for the entire program for the calendar or fiscal year?
- *The Buffer.* What funds are on hand or in reserve? How much money does the church have in unrestricted or unallocated funds and might, if the need arises, be used for operating expenses? Sometimes a church can even borrow some of the restricted funds for emergencies. But the leadership needs to know this number.
- *The Burn.* How much money is spent each month to fulfill ministry commitments? Churches have a "running rate" of money to fund their operations. (Please note the comment below about the Burn.)
- *The Balance.* How much money is needed before the end of the year to pay all the bills? What do we need to have by the end of the year to pay all bills and pay ourselves back (if restricted funds are borrowed)?

In my view, that is it. Any leader aware of these four numbers is "minding the store," as it were. Of course, there are other numbers to consider, such as attendance, membership demographics, etc., but any pastor who does not know the four basic *B*'s for their congregation is flying blind.

A COMMENT ABOUT THE BURN

We need to understand how money flows into a church. Treasurers and finance committee members do too. This is a tricky but true statement about church income and expenses: income seldom equals expenses until the end of year. In the last month of the year, revenue usually exceeds expenses. We should never call December a "black" month, but it normally has the same effect as Black Friday.

This fact of life is the bane of church treasurers and other members of a finance committee. But it is to be expected. Why? By default, we routinely spread expenses out over twelve months of programming. We write checks for our payroll, program costs, and other expenses over twelve months—pretty much the same dollar amount every thirty-day cycle. But income does not come in evenly. The first eleven months donations usually look like blips on a heart-rate monitor—the totals go up and down. Then in December, everyone increases giving to catch up by the end of the year (at least we hope and pray).

Here is a third way to view it (and my favorite way). A church should plan its expenses over twelve months but depend on income to be given over thirteen months—and December is two months. With this simple formula, about which your "mileage may vary," we should know that the church will be underwater for a few months here and there.

HAPPY ST. MATTHEW'S DAY!

September 22 is one of the most ironic days of the year. It is the day after what some Christian traditions observe as the Feast of St. Matthew, named after the tax-collector turned follower of Christ. Many readers of this book may know this, many may not. But many Christians around the world know September 21 as St. Matthew's Day. If you are a pastor, you will not be sorry to learn this date. Why? Read on.

In an ironic accident of timing and calendar, the day *after* the observance of the converted tax-collector is the beginning of a hundred-day, year-end countdown. There are a hundred days of the year left, beginning on September 22. (There is absolutely no spiritual point to be made here; only a practical one.)

In my years as a senior pastor, September 21 marked the moment I needed to get serious about the four *B*'s of the budget and make plans to encourage the membership to help complete the calendar year with strength and momentum. I had exactly a hundred days left until the end of the year starting the very next day.

I can be criticized on this point, I know. I have been promoting the development of stewards, not donors and givers to the church. Indeed, I hope that year after year of teaching and testimonies about stewardship, much of the church had come to know the good news about giving. But our church was constantly bringing in new members who, as I have said earlier, had no habits or bad habits about giving.

In other words, no matter how effective I might have been in teaching (or thought I might have been), I always felt that the last hundred days was an opportunity to sharpen the point and bring more people into an understanding of biblical stewardship. It is probably true of all our congregations: most members need some gentle reminding/nudging/updating and encouragement to give to their congregations in the last months of the year.

BEST PRACTICES FOR YEAR-END GIVING

Over the years of my ministry as the rector of Christ Church in Plano, Texas, and while coaching and counseling young leaders about increasing stewardship and generosity in their church, I have collected a number of best practices to encourage year-end giving in the last hundred days. Some readers may be offended by a few of the ideas and practices––they are too direct or too tacky—but some might be helpful.

Pray. Pastors should regularly pray about the financial health of their churches. This is obvious, but I don't want to leave it unsaid. We need to pray intentionally about every aspect of stewardship. Ask God for wisdom and provision. Seek his guidance to help members grow in the area of generosity. Pray for individuals ahead of any sit-down, face-to-face meeting. We pray alone, but not just alone.

Appeal Letter. Write a year-end letter to everyone in the congregation. This is obvious and should be non-negotiable. We must work on a clear, heartfelt message. We should have much to say. We should convey a sense of thanks and praise for what God has done in the church. And we should be honest about the budget and balance. Let people know exactly how much money the church needs to finish the year in the black.

Year-to-Date Giving Statement. Many churches send out quarterly giving statements. Consider adding one more to the schedule to be sent right after the last Sunday of November. The letter should show members a year-to-date amount given by that individual or family.

Seeing their actual, current numbers helps people know where they stand. Are they on track or falling behind for the year? With this data in hand, they can prayerfully decide how to respond to the year-end letter when it arrives.

A Christmas Wish List. There are two kinds of giving to any church through the year. There are "gifts," which make up most of the giving. These are money donations given for ministry. But there are also "gifts in kind." These are contribution of goods other than cash.

Each staff leader or volunteer in a program area of any congregation has unbudgeted or "wish list" items that they could use and would use if it were in the budget. But often these items are delayed or cut for a variety of reasons.

However, if every child has a "wish list" of items, why not encourage the staff to generate a list of items to help the ministry and further the mission of the church?

This is a fun and effective way to invite people to give tangibly at the end of the year. It incorporates some of the best aspects of the Christmas gift-giving culture and leverages them for the benefit of the Lord.

Give Thanks. Hopefully, as pastors, we say thanks throughout the year. We want to cultivate not only a culture of generosity and but also a heart of gratitude in our church.

We should thank all service attendees and members. But before we think about how to ask for additional giving at the end of the year (which we most often need to do), we should take some time to make sure we acknowledge the people who have helped the church along the way.

Wise pastors might use the Feast of St. Matthew to send out thank-you letters before the appeal letter goes out. I often handwrite letters to some of my key leaders and most generous members—at Thanksgiving. What better time to say thanks?

Tax Benefits. We all know the United States Internal Revenue Service (IRS) allows us to deduct our church donations if we itemize charitable giving on our tax returns. Depending on the income level and other deductions of the individual or couple, this makes sense. Many parishioners take advantage of the provision.

Older congregants have another tax-saving option too. The IRS requires citizens to begin withdrawing from their IRAs at age seventy-two if they have not done so earlier. These withdrawals, as well as stocks, bonds, real estates, and more, can be donated to charities. (Canada allows charitable giving tax credits too.)

As the pastor, it is not our job to be a financial expert or offer qualified money advice. However, we need to be up to speed on the basic giving options, including yearly changes in the law. Then we should educate and explain these tax breaks to our people.

We all can take advantage of IRS charitable giving allowances, but a fine line exists. As pastors, we should never encourage or prod people to give simply to gain a tax break. This mindset is not the best motivation to cultivate a culture of generosity. Biblical giving comes from the heart, not from a government benefit.

Venmo and Zelle. Year-end gifts need to be received by the end of December. Some churches have the treasurer available on site during business hours on New Year's Eve. I installed a lockbox on the entry door to the ministry offices. Don't laugh. Some people wait until the very last minute to give. (I never knew why but one faithful man drove to the church ever New Year's Eve at 11:45 and slid an envelope containing his annual contribution into the lockbox. It was recorded and counted in the year it was given.)

Today we need donation tabs on our websites and giving apps designated for our church. In a world of Venmo and Zelle, we must make sure we can receive one-time gifts and recurring donations electronically. Let's remember, for members of the younger generations (millennials and Gen-Z), making a donation is just a Smartphone tap away.

Face-to-Face. Campaigns, sermons, letters, and technology all help make the year-end giving drive a success. But nothing beats an honest face-to-face conversation. As noted earlier, a meeting is essential when recruiting members to pledge. Most often, these meetings happen between the senior pastor and primary donors in the congregation, but the conversation can and should happen with others too.

Some people in our congregations have the spiritual gift of giving. The Lord brought them to us to exercise that gift on behalf of the whole congregation. Saint Paul wrote about this in Romans 12:6–8:

> *Having gifts that differ according to the grace given to us, let us use them: if prophecy, in proportion to our faith; if service, in our serving; the one who teaches, in his teaching; the one who exhorts, in his exhortation; the one who contributes, in generosity; the one who leads, with zeal; the one who does acts of mercy, with cheerfulness.*

Do not miss what Paul said. Some of our members have the gift of generosity. Pause to think about it; certain members will come to mind. They give cheerfully, sacrificially, and significantly.

A face-to-face conversation should not be looked at as a sales job or even as fundraising. It is a pastoral task to invite those with this spiritual gift to exercise it.

Look Forward Together. Ending the year well positions the church to start the next year well. To that end, during our year-end campaign we may want to emphasize goals for the following year. People always want to move forward in hope. What is on the horizon? What will inspire our members? Thinking about why we need to finish this year strong to get ready for next year can motivate people to give.

We need to build a financial narrative that quickly walks people through our key goals and accomplishments. Remember how the list that St. Archimedes assembled impacted members and the community? We can do the same in our setting. If we have new initiatives coming up in the next year, we should start talking about why the church needs to increase generosity to meet the bold goals.

The end of the year is a great time to talk about what lies ahead, especially if some of the new initiatives start early in the following year.

Model Generosity. One way we can increase year-end giving is to model generosity ourselves—personally and as a congregation. Of course, the staff will work to keep expenses under control, but the members need to see outflow of giving and inflow as well.

Tell your church about whom the congregation has served this year. This starts with practical outflow such as food and counseling. Again, look at the St. Archimedes list for cues.

Did the church invest in frontline outreach efforts and ministry partners? How did the church impact the community? Highlight those things. Show how the church wisely invested the gifts of the congregation for the sake of the Kingdom. Help your members be proud of their church in the best sense of the word. This is not bragging. It is showing your members the breadth and depth of their impact over the year.

Are there other practices and emphases that come to mind when you scan this list. No doubt there are. Use the time allotted between St. Matthew's Day (September 21) and New Year's Eve—the full hundred days—to put the most successful plan and promising ideas into practice.

10

FUNDING CAPITAL PROJECTS OR IMPROVEMENTS

In 1985, I planted a church in Dallas. We started out small, and ably met our initial facility rental costs. As we grew, we required more space. Like any expanding congregation, we needed land and buildings.

Acquiring real estate takes money. Like most congregations, after ministry expenses were met, our checking account balance was close to zero. As I already noted, our vestry constantly examined our options. Curtailing ministry or downsizing staff was not one of them. To take on debt or approach individual major donors to give more had some appeal. But ultimately, the congregation needed to flex its generosity muscles—for both spiritual and practical reasons.

As it turned out, the church I pastored for over three decades ran seven back-to-back capital campaigns! Every three years, we rolled out a new program. We presented fresh ministry needs and opportunities because, well, we have fresh ministry needs and new opportunities. We explained to our members how numerical and outreach increase translated into the need to acquire more land, build more buildings, renovate property, and finally pay off all debt.

For some church members and leaders, the never-ending series of campaigns was too much. They felt that the church's leadership was in a constant state of asking for money. And they were right. But as I expressed to countless people in many sermons, coffee-shop conversations, dinners, and one-on-one meetings, when a family grows, it requires more of everything.

MONEY SOURCES

With growth comes a need for extra funds. Without more funding, a church cannot even dream about permanent projects such as campus expansion, land purchase, and building construction. Furthermore, the funds needed are usually far beyond the ordinary year-to-year expenses of operating the ministry. Gathering the money needed usually requires a specific, extraordinary effort to raise funds to underwrite the project.

I know of only three ways to obtain the needed funds for major projects.

- *Debt.* The church can usually take out a loan and go into debt and complete the project.
- *Donors.* The leaders of the church can approach wealthy and generous donors who could contribute large sums for the project.
- *Drive.* The leaders can take the time to organize a communication campaign to reach everyone in the congregation, asking them to make capital donations for the next two to three years, over and above their regular giving.

The Debt Model. When the church borrows money, like everyone else who gets a loan, it must make payments for years and years to come. Banks have specific requirements to meet and must charge substantial interest. Usually, if the church can make a sufficient down payment, the loaning institution welcomes it as a client. With all due respect, bankers love people (and churches) who owe them money. And the debt arrangement puts the bank in the driver's seat.

The obvious drawback to this model is financial. The church will pay back the loan (principal and interest) over a long time. Since there is no tax advantage to paying interest, the interest paid to the bank is better be used directly for ministry, evangelism, outreach, or missions.

There is another drawback. The debt model doesn't allow God to move on the hearts of the entire congregation. In a debt model, the church leadership makes all the financial decisions without considering the people's willingness, ability, or interest in being a part of the project.

The Donor Model. Another method of raising funds for a capital project is to approach a few committed and wealthy congregation members to fund the project. In our world, financial ability and resources are not distributed equally. Some people have little wealth, and some have a lot. Most people can give something, but only a few can make a large, substantial donation.

The donor model is an effective way to raise funds; however, the people who have the resources must be excited and committed to giving it. But it has the same apparent drawbacks as the debt model: the entire congregation misses out on the opportunity to pray about their financial commitment.

The other drawback to this model is that it assumes that the pastor or the board knows everyone in the church who has significant means. This is never true. People's net worth is a very private thing for most of us. There are families in every church with far more wealth than most people know. And other families in the church have far less than others might guess or assume.

The Drive Model. The third method of raising funds is to design and develop a plan to communicate the opportunity, plan, and financial need with members. After the senior pastor and lay leadership present the vision, everyone has the time and the focus to consider prayerfully his or her level of financial commitment. In this way, the entire congregation gets involved, and every member or committed visitor is asked to make a financial pledge or donation.

A Combination. In truth, for many congregations, the project undertaken will require aspects of all three models. The church launches a capital campaign to invite the entire congregation to consider financial commitments to the project. A capital campaign always involves unique one-on-one conversations with people in the congregation who have the means and the willpower to be significant givers. And finally, the church will most likely work with their local bank or lending institution to provide for bridge loans, cash flow, and other shortfalls.

11

INSIDE A CAPITAL CAMPAIGN

When a church outgrows its rental facilities or sanctuary, it is good news. A positive buzz happens. Excited members feel a common sense of purpose. However, if we are not careful, we can roll out our capital campaign to yawns and assumptions. Of course, a bigger church needs more money. No news there.

An upbeat vibe or hopeful tone helps build on the initial enthusiasm of growth. Every capital campaign needs purpose to bring it to life. The tone should not be just about raising money. Institutions take that approach. The narrative of a church campaign should be to ask God to move in the hearts and minds of every church member to participate in the project as God leads.

A capital campaign is not about fundraising, although money will be raised. It is about commitment and stewardship—the spiritual driving forces behind growth. A campaign is a spiritual endeavor to bring every church member to a prayerful decision about one specific question: What does God want him or her to do for the mission?

This is the only question that matters. When hearing God's call serves as the campaign's centerpiece, the church will be strengthened. The congregation will likely grow in depth and discipleship.

SEVEN ESSENTIALS FOR A SUCCESSFUL CAPITAL CAMPAIGN

When we launch a capital campaign, we need to prepare to work hard. A focus on fundraising can interrupt our month-to-month ministries. Since the campaign should affect everyone, it needs thorough planning. As a veteran of seven of these campaigns, I can give some advice.

Here are the seven essential elements of a successful plan:

1. *A Clear, Compelling Need.* We must present a clear, compelling need that addresses a simple and obvious problem. Bringing in money for a general church budget is one thing. Most people know that tithes fund salaries, programs, and operating costs. And those who give, do so willingly. They accept the practical fact that they do not need to know everything about how every nickel is spent.

Capital funds are different. The church raises them over and above the annual giving. The donor needs a simple explanation. We can write a statement to explain why the church needs the money. Then the leadership teams expound on it in one-to-one conversations, sermons, major presentations, and living room visits.

It is tempting for leadership to combine capital projects, such as mission giving and debt retirement. But frankly, multiple goals tend to cloud the issue. If the church needs to buy land and build a building, then that should be the only purpose of a capital funds campaign.

2. *A Long-Term Vision.* Many leaders know what their church needs. A plot of land enables a young congregation to expand. A refurbished building or a replacement brings new life to an older congregation. A fellowship in debt yearns to be free from mortgage payments. These are all legitimate desires. And each one answers the "what" question for the capital campaign. What are we trying to do?

We need to ask more questions too. Why? Why are launching this project? How? How does it fit into a long-term mission plan for the church? As I mentioned, it might be obvious—and it usually is—that a young church needs to have a permanent home. But the church leadership must be clear about why. What difference will a new sanctuary make for our church and the broader community?

A church must spend the time and effort to formulate and communicate a clear mission purpose. This must happen long before we articulate the need for a specific capital project. It can take years to gain traction, and after members climb on board, the messaging about vision should never stop.

These goals and values can be expressed during member classes, annual vision day teaching, or other specific points on contact. But they should be reinforced all year long in sermons, written communication, and one-on-one encounters. In other words, the church's mission should not be a surprise for the members. They should be acquainted with it as a regular part of their congregational identity.

3. *Comprehensive Engagement.* Everyone in the church must be involved. This takes time and a plan. The larger the congregation, the more effort required.

As any capital campaign worker will acknowledge, it takes multiple efforts and redundant communication to ensure every church member knows a project has been launched. Presumption often lulls leadership into believing that every parishioner stays up to date with all church happenings. They do not! My rule of thumb: about the time the church's leadership grows weary of hearing about the project, the broader membership begins to perk up to the idea!

Therefore, planning must happen. It takes months, not weeks, to get all the details lined up. Meetings must be scheduled, letters written, videos produced, visits made, and sermons prepared.

Another rule of thumb: the simpler the form of communication, the less effective it is. Want an easy way to reach the entire congregation? Send a mass email, of course. It is cheap. It is quick. And it can be accomplished from a desktop or even a smartphone. Eureka! Check it off the list!

But here is a true saying and worthy of all pastors to be believed: the most effective form of communication (face-to-face encounters) is the least efficient. This is the first and greatest truth for all church communication, and the second truth is like it: the most efficient form of communication (email) is the least effective.

At first glance, a mass email sounds like a panacea to our overbooked calendar when we need to reach a large group fast. But the outcome we desire likely will not happen. People scan emails and delete them quickly—if they open them at all. One member of the household may not share an email's content with their spouse. Email does not provide context or personality. There is nothing special about email. They can easily be deleted or hidden in the spam folder. Too many bad scenarios can unfold when we count on emails to be our primary messenger.

To reach the most people with the greatest impact, we must turn to a form of communication that requires the most effort: face-to-face visits. One-on-one or small group presentations are essential.

How much time should we allow for these meetings to occur? It is hard to say precisely, but after my seven back-to-back capital campaigns, most of the efforts took five to six months to plan and execute.

4. *Major Donor Recruitment.* A capital campaign usually requires the senior pastor of the church, and others, to make one-on-one visits with those who have the most substantial capacity to give. The people on this visitation list are not only those who have a high ability to give in real dollars but are also the most committed in giving time and skills to the church.

The people of the world often use money to classify people into status levels. The New Testament writers frowned upon this attitude. Early Christians promoted the ideal of equality among members. Any pastor who segments his or her church members according to monetary potential risks taking on a very worldly perspective.

However, some people can and will give more than others. They have what I have already referred to as the gift of giving. The church's leadership owes it to the congregation to discover those in the church with the means or the gift of giving. As a matter of Christian discipleship, the church should encourage those members to use their gifts for the church's welfare.

Again, I understand the valid concerns pastors and leaders might have about recruiting people according to their giving potential. I was allergic to the idea early on in my ministry. I had to check and double-check my spirit as I approached the more affluent brothers and sisters in the faith. I had to be certain I did not show favoritism to them according to their means.

These are fundamental questions for any pastor, and, for the most part, I felt that I was honest and balanced in my approach.

5. *Influential Lay Leader.* Any capital campaign program should be chaired by one or two people who have demonstrated leadership skills, credibility, and generosity. These brothers and sisters are, in a sense, the face and the voice of the campaign. They must be well-known and trusted in the church.

The chairman must be sold out to the project and invest the time and energy to make it to the finish line. The chair cannot be chosen from the ranks of the reluctant. Too often, churches convey leadership positions on halfhearted people, hoping that they will rise to the task and become committed over time. This is not a good idea. In addition to having a heart for the project, the chairman must have the time. Their role cannot be delegated.

In *Leadership Jazz*, Max DePree writes, "*Leadership is not a position, but a job. It's hard and exciting and good work. It's also serious meddling in other people's lives.*"

What a great quote. It applies to a capital campaign because the chairman or the campaign leader will stand before his or her peers in the congregation and ask them to be generous at a sacrificial level. It is one thing for the pastor to advocate for generosity and sacrificial giving. But the lay leader of the capital campaign models it before the congregation. He or she is one of them. The campaign leader says, "Follow my lead." This, as DePree's quote suggests, meddles in other people's lives—in a good way.

In other words, the chairman doesn't carry an honorary title. He or she must do a lot of work. Committees must be chaired and meetings led. The chairman must take time to delegate work and track the completion of tasks. He or she motivates, oversees, and leads every step of the way.

6. *Time to Fulfill Pledges.* A church solicits gifts for a capital campaign that are over and above regular giving. Pledges are essential. But they must be separate from the annual pledges that members make. Promises to financially support the capital campaign help church leaders plan cash flow and borrowing to begin and complete the project.

Typically, capital gifts are given over a two-to-three-year period, depending on the needs for the money. For example, if a church has approximately two hundred members with an annual budget of $500,000, a capital program might raise a total of $1.5 million given over three years. Or, if a two-year-giving period is chosen, the church would receive an additional $1 million for the project.

Many factors go into setting the time frame of the pledging aspect of a project. The church needs to implement and track communicating, soliciting, recording, and accounting capital gifts over an extended period. A professional consultant can help determine the best schedule.

Ask every household to pledge for a two-to-three-year period (usually three years). The reason for the length of the term gives people time to fulfill a larger pledge. For example, in the first campaign that I led, I knew that my wife and I could afford only $100 a week as an extra gift for the capital project. That was an annual pledge of $5,200 dollars.

However, the church asked members to make three-year pledges, which meant that our total commitment would be $15,600 given over three years. This made sense and seemed far more than we had initially imagined we could give. As more people pledged more money over a more extended period, the church could count on more financial resources committed to the project at hand.

7. *Professional Consultant.* The first six points needed for a capital campaign to succeed seem obvious. But here I raise questions about a debated but vital step: Should we hire a professional consultant to come alongside our leadership team? Do we need experts to advise us and help develop the program?

Many vestries and church boards look at the campaign workload and conclude they can handle it themselves. They often say something like this: "Do we really need someone else coming into our church family and giving us direction? No! We got this."

I have written nothing new in this chapter, only refreshed the obvious. In fact, most congregational boards and leadership teams can come up with a similar list of six or seven essential aspects of a campaign. Point seven would not be on most lists.

However, in my view, churches should seriously consider hiring a consultant. These men or women know how to guide the leaders. They can prioritize neglected or forgotten steps, and then make sure we complete everything in a timely fashion. Their skills often include writing and editing. They can help us determine the right communications tone. Furthermore, they come with an objective standpoint that can help us stay grounded.

Because we pay them a modest fee, they have a way of instilling accountability in the teams of people who volunteer their time on behalf of the campaign. Moreover, a consultant can be a friendly ear for the chairman and the pastor. When problems arise, the experience of the consultant comes in handy.

While not provable, I believe a professionally led capital campaign will yields greater investment among members. They will volunteer more time and give more money.

Finally, a church board usually has only one reason not to hire a consultant: cost. Some wrongly assume that the consultant works on a commission basis and will pressure donations to increase his fee. However, most consultants for church programs do not operate this way. Most receive a small, contracted fee.

I look at it this way: Having a consultant on board is free! The invoiced cost is easily offset by the increased number of pledges and larger donations received.

GOOD NEWS

The need for a capital campaign arises when the church takes on a plan of expansion, renovation, outreach, or another new initiative. It means the church is engaged in its mission, becoming unified around a compelling vision, and members and leaders are giving their time and financial treasure for the church's work. They are increasing their commitment to the mission of Jesus Christ.

In other words, when a church needs a capital campaign, it is good news.

12

BEST PRACTICES OF A GENEROUS CHURCH

We have imagined the outward and public practices of the fictional church St. Archimedes. We envisioned how a fully funded mission could impact the world around it. We read that they preach and teach the gospel of Jesus Christ. May the Lord bless us all and make us leaders and members of a church like that one.

St. Archimedes establishes a high bar. How do we get there? What does a fully functional church look like from the inside? What kinds of principles do the leaders follow? How do they communicate their vision and values to members and visitors? How do they weave the practice of generosity into the fabric of their congregational lives?

Over years of ministry and consulting, I have witnessed what many different congregations do. Some churches practice biblical stewardship. Their members give sacrificially. In fact, in one church, the new member's class specifically teaches the value of generosity. New members discover what the church expects of them. No demands are made, but the goal posts are clearly marked. As a result of this high standard, the congregation is properly funded. Staff receives sufficient, living wages, the church property is well-maintained, and all programs go forward with no financial glitches. Moreover, the church routinely publishes its financial needs and year-to-date balance sheet.

Like St. Archimedes, the churches also serve their communities with outreach. They regularly provide funds to community non-profits. They support missionaries and schools in places such as the inner city or overseas. When a natural disaster strikes anywhere in the county, these churches have the resources to dispatch aid immediately.

Generous churches are a wonder to behold. I have been fortunate to witness firsthand some of the work of these congregation. I have also heard numerous stories about successes. From what I have seen, heard, and done, several best practices have emerged. Here are ten that will improve any church.

1. ***Overcome personal roadblocks.*** As I have written, we must freely, confidently, and frequently talk about financial stewardship from the pulpit, in one-on-one conversations, and in small groups. Money, as we know, is one of the most often mentioned themes in the New Testament—in fact in the entire Bible. But as I have already noted, many of us suffer from a misguided concern: that preaching on stewardship will turn off fragile listeners. It might, of course. But we can disarm our critics with honesty. I often say something like, "You know, it is not easy to speak about money because of so many mixed emotions about it, so please give an ear to my understanding of stewardship from a biblical point of view." Acknowledging common fears or worries wins hearers.

Sometimes a deeper emotion lies behind our reluctance to preach about giving. Could we be afraid of conflict or confrontation? This was a big obstacle for me in my early days as a preacher. I wanted to be liked and respected as a leader, as we all do. I confess that I was addicted to the approval of others more than I was compelled to speak the truth in love. I am not proud of that inner conflict. But I was young and learned to find strength from God. I worked through it. Now I speak about tough topics—not just money—without hesitancy.

We need to come to God with our fears and learn to be upfront about money, or we will never be able to teach our members how to become biblical stewards.

2. *Tell the truth about money.* Generous churches begin by telling the truth about money. The pastor and the governing board report openly and honestly about the year-to-date giving and spending.

Commonly, bad news of a financial deficit is always easy to report. Red ink catches the eye. It motivates reluctant givers to make contributions. After all, the church needs the money. Conversely, some churches do not report positive numbers. Why? Often church leadership mistakenly assumes donors who see positive black numbers will scale back making donations.

Being honest always involves a risk. But I have found that members who give to the work of the church do not give to make a budget look good. Instead, they are compelled by the vision and the ministry of their church. We should celebrate great generosity whenever it occurs.

Churches should strive to make the reporting of financial news—even good news—a routine part of the communication efforts. A simple chart usually suffices to show what the church needs, current giving, expenses, and the difference, if any. How simple is that?

3. *Teach stewardship every year.* People who understand their biblical role as a steward fill generous churches. These members know in their hearts that *"all things come from you, and of your own have we given you"* *(1 Chron. 29:14).*

We give back to God. Disciples understand this deep biblical truth, but living it out does not just happen. People must be taught.

Leaders of generous churches plan a comprehensive emphasis and preaching effort on stewardship every year. They commit to it. Put in on the master calendar. This single, simple act almost always increases our parishioner's level of generosity. I recommend that pastors spend three to four weeks a year teaching on stewardship. One week will not suffice; two weeks will only scratch the surface. We should plan for three to four weeks of focused attention. The pastoral leader and preacher should take responsibility to lead this effort.

Preaching and teaching biblical stewardship is not primarily about fundraising. Rather, we broaden the focus. We help our members clarify their personal values and beliefs about ownership, material possessions, and the seductive lures of the world.

Some people may think that pastors teach about stewardship to gather more income. Yes, that is true. But we also cultivate a culture of generosity to address one of the most insidious, ever-present, and pernicious traps that every believer struggles with daily in the Western world: idolatry.

John Calvin wrote in *The Institutes of Christian Religion*: "*The human heart is a perpetual idol factory.*" Calvin drives home the point that each of us dream up and trust enticing things of our own making. We do not tend to worship a stone idol in a makeshift shrine in our homes, but a shiny metal idol with four wheels in our driveway tempts us. Instead of relying upon God for our identity and hope, we easily shift our affections to material possessions.

Calvin's words have never been truer than today. Each of us struggles in this arena. We all live in a world packed full of snares of attraction and affection. As church leaders, we should see our culture's fixation on material possessions as modern examples of idolatry. Preaching and teaching on stewardship on a regular basis will help our people take notice of the idols in their own lives and shift their hearts to biblical generosity.

4. *Invite laity to tell their stories.* Whenever possible, I share from the pulpit the good news of generosity from my own perspective. I always seek to be transparent about what my wife and I do in our giving to the local parish. My stories show that I am walking the talk, not just teaching a concept. My honesty gains the trust of my church members. We connect on a practical level as we seek to live out biblical truths.

As important as it is for me to talk about my struggles and breakthroughs, lay testimonies always prove to be better motivators. One honest parishioner told me after a lay testimony (which followed my own), "The story they told about their commitment was inspiring. Yours was great too, but we sort of pay you to be generous." That is not exactly how it works, but his words stuck in my mind. The laity have great stories, so let them share.

5. *Write a narrative budget.* At the church I served, we often would take our annual year-to-date giving and write a story about it. We went beyond the numbers and the columns of a cold report to describe what we could do because of people's giving. This helped donors see the impact. We called it a "narrative budget."

With a narrative budget we can tell our church's story. Include pictures. Describe the lives that have been touched and changed. Be specific. Describe how the most practical work happens—how does the pastor and staff minister each week? How does giving empower God's work? We can uplift members and even bring tears of joy to their eyes when they see how much impact has been made.

What about the more basic and boring expenses like overhead? I contend that a fully functioning church has no "overhead." A secular business will list staff costs, electric bills, carpet cleaning, administrative costs, and the like in the overhead column. But if we regard the church as the people and the staff and members as the delivery system of ministry to others, there really is no such thing as overhead! Everything is being used for the mission purpose of fulfilling the God-given vision of the congregation.

Honesty is disarming. Stories are engaging. Fear can be overcome. These are just a few of the themes that a church can embrace and begin cultivating a culture of generosity.

6. *Motivate people with joy.* Never write a desperate negative letter to church members asking for money. Never complain about how little people give, how massive a church debt may be, or how expenses have exceeded the initial budget. And never threaten to lay off staff, decrease outreach, or close the doors without a sudden windfall from reluctant givers.

Shame, guilt, and fear may bring in more donations on a limited basis, but they never kickstart a culture of biblical generosity. Why? True biblical stewards do not give because of fear or guilt. They give for reasons of faith, worship, hope, and joy. Christian generosity produces joy! Paul reminds the Corinthians, "*God loves a cheerful giver*" (2 Cor. 9:7).

Over years and years of mistakes and missteps, I have developed a promise-oriented approach to stewardship and generosity. I preach biblical principles and try to show people where embracing this truth will lead them. What kind of life does the Bible promise when we practice what it says? What joy can we expect when we give out of a willing and generous heart?

The Apostle Paul did not use shame or guilt when he reminded the Corinthians to fulfill their pledge commitment. He motivated them with a story about the Macedonian churches. Paul prodded, "You guys are behind. You need to step it up like the Macedonian churches have" (2 Cor. 8:1, author's paraphrase). There was a slight edge to Paul's words, but the tone was uplifting. The apostle talked about the Macedonians' joy, hope, promise, and abundance to spur the Corinthian church into action.

No guilt; just joy.

7. *Use humor.* Most Christians fall woefully short of the biblical stewardship model. To be honest, they even fail to meet their personal giving goals. They are not being faithful. They already know it. We as pastors know it. All have sinned, especially when it comes to generosity.

We want to turn on the light, so our members grasp holistic giving. But how? Most members start in a hole. Scolding them will not help. Pressure backfires. And as noted above, guilt and shame only create a defensive wall around the human heart. How do we break through?

King Solomon offered a tip. He wrote, *"A soft answer turns away wrath, but a harsh word stirs up anger"* (Prov. 15:1). What wisdom! A soft answer.

In my experience, there is no better way to soften the heart than to use humor. In preaching and teaching, banter can blunt the edges of bad news. But well-timed levity can open the heart to receive the good news of leading a generous life. Humor, when spoken in love, will diffuse anxiety and any residual ennui in a congregation.

If we read the Bible, we will find humor there. Even in unlikely passages. Consider this: perhaps we hear the story of the rich man and Lazarus (see Luke 16:19–31) with too-serious ears. The first-century audience might have hooted out loud and slapped their knees at the reversal of fortunes of the main characters. It is the poor man who makes it big in the Kingdom and the rich man who ends up in Hades. The lesson is clear: be generous.

How about the story of the widow's mite? Isn't it a bit wry? No doubt it happened exactly as described in Mark 12:41–44. But the story is bathed in irony. The rich Pharisees liked to trumpet their giving, but here they were outclassed by the poor widow who gave all she had.

My point is that human, earthy stories and truths about generosity have a partnership. They fit together.

8. ***Train the leadership board.*** We must establish biblical generosity as the standard of leadership for our board. There are usually denominational requirements about who can serve in the leadership roles of the church. They must, for example, be a member of the congregation. That makes sense. Of course. But that is a low bar.

It makes better sense to train every nominee or potential candidate before the congregational election or appointment. Let the candidates know what the church expects of board or committee members. Allow them to opt in or out after they count the cost (see Luke 14). Proactively teach biblical stewardship to all prospective candidates. Let them know what it means to serve in leadership.

Then ask each potential board or committee member: "Do you grasp the vision of tithing and sacrificial giving? Will you present your life and your labor to the Lord in meaningful, sacrificial, and generous ways?"

When I served as the rector of an Anglican church, every year for four weeks before our vestry elections, I gathered nominees together on a Saturday morning. During the meeting, I laid out the vision for the parish, the vestry's role, the rector's function, and a few relevant bylaws and canons.

I also made sure to present nominees with the basic biblical principles on stewardship. To serve in leadership, they had to support them. I distributed a policy statement on giving and generosity. Everyone had a choice—to support or not. Some people removed their names from consideration. They counted the cost and decided to pull back. I fully respected their decision. But those who stayed in the process and were elected knew the expectations.

As I have already noted, the rector or pastor is responsible for this training.

9. *Have a plan.* Whether through an annual pledge card system, preaching series, an all-church communication campaign, or something else, we need to have a generosity plan. Whatever system the church decides to use, pledges or non-pledges, intentionality truly matters. Remember, this isn't just about money, rather; it is about discipleship. We are inviting people to participate with us in the mission of God, and we are asking them to relate to money in a radically different, counter-cultural way. We must be intentional, prayerful, and wise to discern whether the annual pledge card system is the best way to do this in our own ministry context.

Pastor, what is your plan for the coming year?

10. *Be generous.* Be generous on every occasion possible. Our example establishes our leadership on stewardship and helps form the DNA of our church. Generosity begets generosity. There is no question about that (see Luke 6:38). Leaders will realize the power of modeling biblical stewardship as they start to act generously. Not surprisingly, the act of generosity on the part of the leader will be productive. It motivates, models, encourages, and shows others how to give.

The topic of stewardship and giving is essential; often, leaders simply need a fresh approach. Hopefully, these ten ideas will help us build a base on which to develop a culture of generosity.

CREATING A CULTURE OF GENEROSITY

I served as the founding pastor of a church for thirty-one years. One of the most amazing features of this congregation was its radical generosity. The people gave. They saw dozens of opportunities to give to our church and beyond our church. It was a joy to lead that parish family and to see what their expansive, effective generosity accomplished. No doubt, Christ Church had a culture of generosity.

I know when it began. Since I was there from the start, I can pinpoint the occasion when the DNA gene was established. Allow me a quick story about the incredible power of a generous example.

When Fran and I were ready to start Christ Church, we were a family of four. When new people came into the worship service as visitors, they met me. I, along with many others, was a full-time greeter. But when they met my wife, Fran, they noticed something about her that was as obvious as it was wonderful. She was pregnant with our third child. He became the first baby born at the new church plant.

In the first few months of church, as people attended and people came to know each other, some of the women worked behind the scenes to hold a baby shower for Fran. They fixed the date of the shower with

Fran and then handed out invitations to the party the following Sundays.

When Fran looked at the printed invitation that had been circulated widely, it suddenly struck her: she (and our newborn) would be the guests of honor and receive gifts upon needed gifts. She was very uncomfortable with that. She told me it was too much. We didn't need all those blankets and cribs, strollers, diapers, bottles, diaper pails, car seats, and other baby paraphernalia.

I assured her that we did! Our finances were very tight, and we could not afford most of those things easily. I was pleased with the prospects of this baby shower because, for our family, it was a windfall. But Fran was very sure—even adamant—that she should not be the recipient. Instead, she wanted to use the occasion of the baby shower to build up the many items needed for the new church nursery. Future babies and infants and future moms would benefit.

We had, what we call today, "rigorous fellowship" about the subject. However, as you might guess, in the end, she prevailed. She changed the invitation to redirect the giving toward the needy nursery for the church. She worked with a few ladies to create a gift registry for the newly redirected party. You can imagine the response. It was overwhelming.

We were fine too, by the way. We were blessed with a bit of the overflow from that party, but in the end, God provided for us as well.

As I look back on the early days of our church and I search for a reasons why it became a church of generous givers—people who would one day build all the buildings we needed, fund missions work, support church plants, deploy a great staff, and give generously to outreach projects in our community—I go back to the day and time of this baby shower. I think Fran set the tone. I think her example created a direction toward and an expectation of generosity.

That is one early example of generosity that helped foster and create a culture of giving. There were dozens, if not hundreds more. In the life of a church there are so many teachable moments like this. As pastors and church leaders, we should look for them and give people the opportunity to choose to be generous.

13

WHY GENEROSITY?

I wrote this field guide to encourage church leaders and pastors to consider how to lead a church toward generosity. There are things to see and do along the journey that will take time, planning, insight, wisdom, knowledge, and prayer. That's why I call this book a field guide. It is intended to you help navigate this journey.

Some aspects of teaching and preaching on biblical stewardship need little explanation. We all know the practical needs for every congregation: the church must pay its bills. That alone motivates some pastors to pay attention to stewardship. But a better, deeper reason for stewardship teaching cuts to the core of our faith. Generosity helps build the foundation of a rich life in Christ.

It is not too bold to say it this way: If a person loves Jesus and seeks to pursue Him as Lord, in time, with teaching, training, and trusting, they will become generous. Following Jesus has a halo effect. It changes us. The Holy Spirit changes our wants and desires about possessions and the hold they can have on us.

But it is even stronger to flip this statement: if a person is not generous, they cannot sustain a complete love and relationship with Jesus. Giving comes with following the Lord. Remove generosity, and we return to our love affair with ourselves and our possessions. Then what we have and hold in our life are only the inert things of the world that do not bring life.

Every church promotes stewardship at some level. Some churches are adept and practiced at it. They have spent years building a culture of generosity, raising money for their mission, giving resources, providing financial relief for others, building their program, and helping members invest in the future.

Some churches rarely mention budgets or money. Some stumble through awkward apologies about it being that time of year again. Sadly, these churches have disconnected stewardship from discipleship. They raise funds because they need money, but the joy of generosity and the blessing from giving are closely held secrets known only by a few.

When we read the New Testament, the early believers were generous, almost beyond our imagination. Their lives (see Acts 2) reflected the life of Jesus. One of their most famous converts, the Apostle Paul, was a generous leader. These lives of generosity should inspire us to help us refocus the emphases in our own congregations.

The life and character of the Early Church was not programmed like our churches are today. We have courses, seminars, and workshops on various Christian lifestyle values and goals. We have curricula on how to evangelize our neighbors. We have very entertaining video lessons that teach the Bible and help people grow in their faith. We have mission trips. We have outreach and service programs. All these are good and wonderful, and our churches need to help Christian members practice and deepen their faith. But there appears to be next-to-no programming like this in the New Testament. A six-week course on how we should share the Gospel seems conspicuous by its absence in the New Testament. Choirs and concerts were not part of the life of the church.

Instead, the heart and center of the Early Church was generosity and generous living. Ministers and pastors today can preach many different sermons and topics from the first few pages of the Acts of the Apostles, but the singular characteristic of the early believers was that they gave. As I read it, giving time and treasure was one of the earliest changes in living and lifestyle that new Christians were asked to make. In love and obedience to Christ, the first Christians imitated the life of Jesus: they gave.

I have become persuaded that the Early Church had something going for it that has been overlooked or downplayed today: they had an overwhelming commitment to give as God has given to them. Further, under the power of the Holy Spirit, their commitment to generosity caused the Early Church to succeed against all odds. They were givers—of time and resources—even when giving made no sense in the broader culture (and it didn't!). Their generosity and commitment to serve generously created a magnetic attraction that drew believers by the thousands.

I hope that this book, *A Field Guide for Giving*, has helped you strengthen your understanding of the role and impact of generosity on your congregation and its mission.

Made in United States
Orlando, FL
14 January 2023